HERO OF FLIGHT 93

HERO OF FLIGHT 93

MARK BINGHAM

BY JON BARRETT

Advocate
BOOKS

MANUFACTURED IN CANADA.

THIS TRADE PAPERBACK ORIGINAL IS PUBLISHED BY ADVOCATE BOOKS,
AN IMPRINT OF ALYSON PUBLICATIONS,
P.O. BOX 4371, LOS ANGELES, CALIFORNIA 90078-4371.
DISTRIBUTION IN THE UNITED KINGDOM BY TURNAROUND PUBLISHER SERVICES LTD.,
UNIT 3, OLYMPIA TRADING ESTATE, COBURG ROAD, WOOD GREEN,
LONDON N22 6TZ ENGLAND.

FIRST EDITION: SEPTEMBER 2002

02 03 04 05 06 ✳ 10 9 8 7 6 5 4 3 2 1

ISBN 1-55583-780-8

LIBRARY OF CONGRESS CATALOGING-IN-PUBLICATION DATA
BARRETT, JON.
    HERO OF FLIGHT 93 : MARK BINGHAM / JON BARRETT.—1ST ED.
    ISBN 1-55583-780-8
        1. BINGHAM, MARK, 1970–2001. 2. GAY HEROES—UNITED STATES—BIOGRAPHY.
3. RUGBY FOOTBALL PLAYERS—UNITED STATES—BIOGRAPHY. 4. UNITED AIRLINES
FLIGHT 93 HIJACKING INCIDENT, 2001. 5. SEPTEMBER 11 TERRORIST ATTACKS, 2001.
I. TITLE: MARK BINGHAM. II. TITLE.
HQ75.8.B56 B37 2002
305.38'9664'092—DC21
[B]   2002027705

CREDITS
• FRONT COVER PHOTOGRAPHY © MATT HALL.
• BACK COVER PHOTOGRAPHY © PAUL HOLM.
• INTERIOR PHOTOGRAPHS COURTESY OF ALICE HOGLAN, UNLESS OTHERWISE NOTED.
• COVER DESIGN BY MATT SAMS.

To Alice Hoglan
and to my own parents

THE FIESTA WAS REALLY STARTED. It kept up day and night for seven days. The dancing kept up, the drinking kept up, the noise went on. The things that happened could only have happened during a fiesta. Everything became quite unreal finally and it seemed as though nothing could have any consequences. It seemed out of place to think of consequences during the fiesta. All during the fiesta you had the feeling, even when it was quiet, that you had to shout any remark to make it heard. It was the same feeling about any action. It was a fiesta and it went on for seven days.

—*The Sun Also Rises,* Ernest Hemingway

OLIVER SIPPLE DIDN'T SET OUT TO become a hero on Sept. 22, 1975. And he certainly didn't set out to become a gay hero. But heroism is seldom a calculated business, and the mantle is most often placed upon those whose extraordinary actions are prompted by unexpected circumstances.

By almost every measure, Sipple had already lived a heroic life when he woke up in his San Francisco home that crisp autumn morning. The 33-year-old, known as Billy to his friends and family, was a Marine Corps veteran who had been twice wounded while serving in the Vietnam War. It wasn't until that afternoon, though, when he headed down to Union Square to catch a glimpse of President Gerald Ford, that his bravery caught the attention of an entire nation.

Sipple was among the thousands of gawkers gathered out-side the St. Francis Hotel when President Ford left the build-ing, undoubtedly a part of the patriotic frenzy that swept the street at that moment. But he stopped going with the flow of the flag-waving crowd the instant its cheers were pierced by a .38 caliber gunshot. Rather than cower or jump for cover, as is most people's instinct in such an emergency, Sipple saw that the gunwoman, Sara Jane Moore, was within his reach, and took action. In the seconds between Moore's first shot and what could have been her second, Sipple shoved her, hard enough to ruin her aim and ensure the president's safety.

America had a new hero. And because he was a gay man living a gay life in a burgeoning gay mecca during the height of the gay liberation movement, activists were eager to claim him as their own. Among those activists was a friend Sipple had known for more than a decade, Castro Camera storeowner Harvey Milk. In the heat of his second unsuccessful bid for the San Francisco Board of Supervisors at the time, Milk decided to sell out Sipple—to out him in the press, essentially. He did so for at least two reasons: It made good press, and he thought President Ford was dragging his feet in officially thanking his friend. Besides, Milk thought, who could better dispel any stereotypes Americans had regarding homosexuality than a gay Marine who had saved the president's life? "For once we can show that gay people do heroic things," Milk is quoted as saying in Randy Shilts's biography of him, *The Mayor of Castro Street*. "It shows that we do good things, not just all that ca-ca about molesting children and hanging out in bathrooms."

Herb Caen of *The San Francisco Chronicle* was the first journalist to mention Sipple's sexual orientation in print, and he did it in a roundabout way. "One of the heroes of the day, Oliver 'Bill' Sipple, the ex-Marine who grabbed Sara Jane Moore's arm just as her gun was fired and thereby may have saved the president's life, was the center of midnight attention at the Red Lantern, a Golden Gate Ave. bar he favors," Caen wrote, without mentioning that the Red Lantern was a gay bar. He continued, "The Rev. Ray Broshears, head of the Helping Hands center, and Gay Politico Harvey Milk, who claim to be among Sipple's close friends, describe themselves as 'proud—maybe this will help break the stereotype.' Sipple is among the workers in Milk's campaign for supe." Anyone familiar with the Red Lantern or, more likely, with Milk's campaign got the message.

Other newspapers were less subtle. Sipple was called a "Homosexual Hero" by the *Chicago Sun-Times* and a "Gay Vet" by the *Denver Post*. His family, who knew nothing about Sipple's sexual orientation before reading about it in *The Detroit News*, disowned him. His mother said she couldn't leave her home without being harassed. And when she died in 1979, Sipple's father barred his gay son from the funeral. Sipple's relatively carefree life had changed for the worse in almost as little time as it had taken him to save the life of the president.

Through it all, Sipple maintained that he was not a gay hero but a hero who happened to be gay. "My sexual orientation has nothing at all to do with saving the president's life," he told reporters. "Just as the color of my eyes or my race has nothing to do with what happened in front of the St. Francis Hotel." To that point, he sued the *Chronicle* and six other newspapers for $15 million, claiming they had violated his right to privacy by reporting his sexual orientation. The court, however, ruled that Sipple lost that right when he saved the president's life and, as a result, became a public figure. Today *Sipple v. Chronicle Publishing Co.* is a staple case lesson in journalism classrooms across the country.

Despite being a court-determined public person, Sipple spent the rest of his life alone in a Tenderloin apartment, sub-sisting on his meager military pension. When he died on Jan. 19, 1989, a full two weeks passed before anyone realized he was gone. The American hero was found lying in bed with a bottle of bourbon at his side. His apartment walls were covered with newspaper clippings that recounted his heroism and with the framed thank-you letter sent from the White House on Sept. 25, 1975, the day after Sipple's sexual orientation was first reported in the *Chronicle*.

"I want you to know how much I appreciated your selfless actions last Monday," the letter read. "The events were a shock to us all, but you acted quickly and without fear for your own safety. By doing so, you helped to avert danger to me and to others in the crowd. You have my heartfelt appreciation." —President Gerald Ford

The often-virulent reaction Sipple received when the public learned he was gay reflected the cultural tug-of-war taking place in the United States at the time. Almost every sizable win on the part of gay people in the late 1970s was met with an equally large retaliation. For example, when Harvey Milk was elected to the Board of Supervisors in 1976, only two years passed before he and Mayor George Moscone were gunned down by former supervisor Dan White. The assassinations were considered the largest attack on the gay community before the beginning of the HIV/AIDS crisis several years later. Similarly, in Florida's Dade County, gay activists won a groundbreaking victory when the county commission passed a human rights ordinance in January 1977. Then, just six months later, former Miss America runner-up and orange juice spokeswoman Anita Bryant convinced the county's voters to repeal the ordinance. Her "Save the Children" campaign helped launch what we know today as the far-right movement, headed by the likes of Jerry Falwell and Pat Robertson.

Mark Bingham was only 7 years old in 1977. And though he was living in the shadow of Miami's Orange Bowl at the time, it's highly unlikely that he heard any of the back and forth between gay activists and Bryant. If he did, it's unlikely that he paid much attention to it. But 24 years later, Mark was reaping the benefits of those battles and others like them. Gay people in San Francisco didn't have to fight so hard to get a representative on the Board of Supervisors because it now had one as its president. And while those in Miami were still struggling over legislated protections on the county level, there is little doubt that they were close to winning the two-decade-long war. Miami was now a destination for open-minded people from around the world, while Bryant, long ago branded as little more than a hairsprayed holy roller, was filing for bankruptcy in Sevier County, Tenn.

Mark's life had little in common with Oliver Sipple's. As a young man, Sipple had moved to San Francisco because it was one of the few places where he could truly be himself—by losing himself in a gay ghetto. Mark wanted nothing to do with the ghettoized life. San Francisco didn't serve as a beacon for him as it had to so many others. He lived there by default, for the most part. His family had moved to the Bay Area in the early 1980s, and most of them were still there. Mark had gay friends and he had straight friends and he was out to most all of them—just as he was to most of his family and business associates. Mark wasn't a gay activist either, and he didn't trouble himself with what are considered the gay issues of the day. Because of where he lived and because of the civil rights victories won by those who had lived in San Francisco before him, he really didn't have to. As much as Sipple wanted the public to believe he was a hero who just happened to be gay, Mark lived his life very much like a man who just happened to be gay.

That's the way things were Sept. 11, 2001. No one at Newark International Airport knew Mark's sexual orientation when he bounded onto United Airlines Flight 93 that morning. He didn't know the sexual orientation of the other 43 passengers and crew onboard—and very likely didn't think much about it. Still, when Americans learned of the efforts that the passengers and crew on that plane took to ensure that the Boeing 757—the last of the four planes hijacked by terrorists that morning—didn't hit its intended target, they wanted to know about these new heroes. And it wasn't long before Mark's sexual orientation played a bigger part in the headlines than it ever had in his life. As they had done close to three decades before with Sipple, activists trumpeted his name—for here was another man who shattered still-thriving gay stereotypes. And as the president of his own company and a national collegiate championship rugby player, Mark was more than palatable to the increasingly diversity-conscious media. There's no question that the press treated Mark's story differently than they did Sipple's. Instead of printing "Homosexual Hero" stories, newspapers such as *The New York Times* ran headlines that asked "Gay Hero, or Hero Who Was Gay?" Nevertheless, the "gay hero" moniker stuck.

Mark, like Oliver Sipple, didn't set out to become a hero that morning. He didn't know his actions would be credited for saving the White House or the U.S. Capitol—or that he would be among the first men and women called to fight in a war he didn't even know existed. And had he survived, Mark probably would have fought as fervently as Sipple had to make people understand that despite his heroism he was no different than anyone else. He wouldn't have considered the press coverage of his sexual orientation a violation of privacy, but he would have reiterated Sipple's point—that his homosexuality had no more a role to play in his actions that morning than did his eye color or race. What is more important, he would have said, is that he simply understood the difference between right and wrong.

But the burden of getting that message out now rests with Mark Bingham's friends and loved ones—many of whose stories are told in the following pages. And as much as they recognize that Mark's story and his status as a "gay hero" will help eliminate the same harmful stereotypes that left Oliver Sipple banned from his own mother's funeral, they're determined to make sure that the true story of the man they loved isn't lost in the shadow of a man who really never existed.

"Hey, Mark, this is Dad. Just calling to see how you're doing. Looking at that big wreck, man. I hope you're not too close to that. So [pause and muffled sobs] give me a call when you can. Bye."

"Hey, Mark, Amanda. Where are you? Call me, please. Bye."

"Hi, Mark. This is Judy. I don't know if you're flying or what because I just heard that all the plane traffic has been grounded today after the attack in New York and Washington.... I just would like to know if you're in the air or what's happening. It's very worrying with these things. Anyway, talk to you soon. Thanks. Bye."

—the first three unheard voice-mail messages left on Mark Bingham's mobile phone on Sept. 11, 2001—the first from his father, Jerry Bingham; the second from his friend and New York City roommate, Amanda Mark; and the third from his colleague Judy Curtis

MARK BINGHAM HAD A LOT on his mind that Tuesday morning. Not only was he supposed to fly home to San Francisco to serve as an usher at a fraternity brother's wedding, but he was going to spend the next few days mulling over the future of his public relations firm, The Bingham Group. Since starting the eponymous operation in a shared San Francisco loft space in 1999, Mark had watched business in the dot-com world explode. And his company rode the E-business boom for all it was worth—counting some of the biggest corporations in the industry, including 3Com, among its clients. Just as young 20- and 30-somethings throughout the Bay Area were comparing their stock options and planning for early retirements, The Bingham Group was well placed to take advantage of the millions of dollars these wundercompanies wanted to spend on public relations and strategic planning services.

By May 2000, The Bingham Group had moved into its own office on San Francisco's Lafayette Street; in March 2001 the company announced the opening of a Manhattan office. "Our New York office allows us to be closer to the professional communities we work with daily—not just here in the United States but in Europe as well," Mark wrote in a press release that spring. "TBG plans to take advantage of new business opportunities in New York's hotbed of wireless, content, and broadband entertainment companies, which are congruent with TBG's proven record of media penetration." Truth be told, The Bingham Group's Manhattan office consisted solely of Mark and could count no clients of its own. But with the success Mark had had in California's Silicon Valley, there was no reason to think he couldn't be a major player in New York's Silicon Alley too.

No amount of optimism, however, could stop the dot-com world from tanking as suddenly as it did that summer of 2001. And now, fresh from laying off all but two of The Bingham Group's employees, Mark had to figure out what to do next.

So yes, Mark Bingham had a lot on his mind that Tuesday morning. Yet, at 7:42 A.M., when his friend Matt Hall dropped him off outside Terminal A at Newark International Airport, all Mark could think about was making his 8 A.M. flight. A seasoned traveler—not to mention the son of a United Airlines flight attendant—Mark knew he was cutting it close. In fact, he knew he would be more than lucky if the door to the plane was still open when he reached the gate. But he also knew how to avoid the obstacles that could trip up a less-frequent flyer. As he approached the security checkpoint, he probably already had shuffled his spare change from his pockets, taken care of his cell phone, and determined the shortest and fastest line. So after both he and his Cal-Berkeley bag quickly passed inspection, the 6-foot-4, 220-pound man most likely threw the duffel over his shoulder and barreled down the crowded corridor to Gate 17, down the jet bridge, and into his seat, 4D. He made it just seconds before the gate agent closed the door to the Boeing 757, and as fate would have it, he was the last passenger to board United Airlines Flight 93.

Anyone who knew Mark wouldn't be surprised that he had made it on the plane that morning; he wasn't the kind of guy who let anything stand in his way. Stories abound about his determination on the rugby field, as a member of both his high school team in Los Gatos, Calif., and a national championship–winning Cal team. Always one of the tallest guys on his team, Mark usually played forward, what his friends say is one of the most injury-prone positions on the field. But he loved the game so much he didn't worry much about what it might do to his body—unless you count the times he wrapped electrical tape around his ears so they wouldn't get ripped off his head in the heat of a brutal scrum.

He was bold off the field too, as was the case one afternoon when he and his roommate Amanda Mark found themselves up against police barricades during a film shoot in Manhattan's Union Square. "The next thing I knew, Mark took my hand and we were on the other side of the barricades and someone was asking us if we were with the film crew," Amanda remembers. Mark nodded his head to indicate that they were with the crew and then strode immediately over to Tom Cruise, who was in the middle of shooting the feature film *Vanilla Sky*. "Nice to meet you, Mr. Cruise," he said confidently as he shook the movie star's hand. And friends can't forget Mark's unconventional yet ultimately successful attempt to get a bird's-eye view from New York's Chrysler Building, his favorite in the city. Since the art deco landmark's observatory has been closed for decades, Mark rode the elevator until he saw a woman get off at a dentist's office on the 69th floor and heard the receptionist say, "Hello, Rose." After a few more minutes riding the elevator, Mark himself got off on the 69th floor and proceeded to gawk at the magnificent and otherwise off-limits views from the dentist's office. When a member of the dentist's staff asked if he needed any help, a nonchalant Mark said, "I'm just waiting for my Aunt Rose."

"Most people go through life with a certain set of boundaries that keep them from doing things that might get them in trouble," Mark's friend Dave Kupiecki says. "Mark always seemed to look past those boundaries. He saw something he wanted to do and he did it."

Now that Mark was actually on the plane, he could give his

signature determination a rest. He accepted a glass of orange juice from the flight attendant and at 7:49 A.M. called his friend Matt, who by this time was cruising down Interstate 78 on his way to work. "Thanks for driving so crazy to get me here," Mark said quickly. "I've made the plane and I'm sitting in first class. And I'm drinking a glass of orange juice." Then, faced with a five-and-a-half-hour flight and at least that much time to contemplate all that awaited him in San Francisco, Mark had a chance to catch his breath, relax, and wait for takeoff.

The span of time between when passengers board an airplane and when the plane actually takes off is one of those rare periods in life of true limbo—a forced time-out when, even if you have business to conduct, the Federal Aviation Administration requires that you turn off your mobile phone, your laptop computer, your Palm Pilot, and even your personal stereo. Some people spend this time alternately checking their watches and shaking their heads in frustration. Others dig into the seat pocket in front of them and flip through the obligatory catalog, perhaps wondering if there really is a market for cascading water dishes for cats. Still others are lulled to sleep by the warm rays beating in through the aircraft's side windows—sometimes not waking up until after the plane is in the air, shaking their heads in disbelief that they really slept through takeoff.

For Mark, a social charmer if there ever was one, this was often his chance to sweet-talk the flight attendants. Holland Carney, a former boss of Mark's who took many business trips with him, remembers that her colleague had an endless appetite for both conversation and food and that he didn't shy away from chatting up the on-flight crew so that they might give him an extra meal later on. Tuesday morning provided ample time for all of that. Traffic on Newark's runways was more delayed than usual, and Flight 93 didn't leave the gate until 8:30 A.M.—a full 41 minutes after Mark had called Matt to let him know he had made it onto the flight.

The delay probably gave Mark an opportunity to introduce

himself to Tom Burnett, who was sitting in his row. Like Mark, Tom was a big man—the 38-year-old stood 6 feet tall and weighed close to 200 pounds. But the men were similar in more ways than just their stature. Both called Northern California home (Tom lived in San Ramon), both were related to a flight attendant (Tom's wife, Deena, once flew for Delta Air Lines), and both were avid sportsmen (Tom had been the quarterback on his high school football team). There's little question that the two of them would have found plenty to talk about. And Tom of all people would have appreciated and understood the enthusiasm Mark exuded if they had a chance to discuss the previous few days Mark had spent attending tennis matches at the U.S. Open.

Mark had purchased box-seat tickets (for a men's quarterfinal match) on eBay as a birthday present for Amanda. There was an unspoken rivalry between the two when it came to birthday surprises. Amanda had been the reigning champion; she had flown from her native Sydney to arrive unannounced in San Francisco for Mark's 30th birthday on May 22, 2000. But Mark was determined to outdo her on her 31st birthday, September 9. Nevertheless, his element of surprise was ruined when, a week prior to the Open, Amanda announced she would be attending a match with some of her colleagues at Morgan Stanley. The news forced a disappointed Mark to spill the beans about his plan.

Evidently, the missing element of surprise didn't spoil Mark's recipe for fun. On September 6, he and Amanda headed to Arthur Ashe Stadium in Flushing Meadows, Queens, where 19-year-old American Andy Roddick took on 20-year-old Australian Lleyton Hewitt. As might be expected, the crowd was solidly behind Roddick throughout the match, which lasted an unusually long three hours and 40 minutes. At times, in fact, the stadium erupted with chants of "USA, USA." However, it being Amanda's birthday and all, Mark literally wrapped himself up in the Australian flag and, with Amanda's help, became the cheering section for the Aussie, who went on to win the match. Things were tense on the court that night, escalating to the point where a frustrated Roddick called the umpire a moron, but the mood couldn't have been more celebratory in Amanda and Mark's box. "We got everyone around us drinking piña coladas with an extra shot of rum," Amanda says, laughing. "It was just raucous."

The real surprise for them both came September 8, when Mark scored three tickets—for himself, Amanda, and their friend Larry Salmela—to the women's final match between sisters Venus and Serena Williams. The match was short—21-year-old Venus essentially stomped on 19-year-old Serena, beating her in just two sets—and their seats weren't quite as good this time. But the trio didn't have any less fun than Mark and Amanda had had two nights prior. "We were in the second row from the top of the stadium, definitely the nosebleed section," Larry says. "But when the match was over and they were doing the award ceremony Mark said, 'We've got to get down there.' So we charged through security and got close enough to the Williams sisters that we were able to get pictures of us with them getting their trophies in the background."

Ticketless on Sunday, September 9, which was Amanda's actual birthday, the roommates and several of their friends gathered at one of Mark's favorite bars, the Riviera Café in Greenwich Village, to watch the men's finals match between Hewitt and Pete Sampras. Mark and Amanda again threw their very vocal support behind the Aussie even though, as was the case in Flushing Meadows three days earlier, they were far outnumbered at the Riviera by supporters for the American, Sampras. And again, just as it had Thursday night, something clicked for Hewitt, who ended up walking away with the title.

Hewitt was seeded fourth in the tournament and was hardly an underdog, but Mark and Amanda, like any true sports fans, couldn't help but think they had something to do with his triumph. And if Amanda's birthday wasn't reason enough to celebrate that night, Hewitt's victory gave them an excuse to really tie one on. Bloody Marys at the Riviera led to shots of Jagermeister at Fiddlesticks Pub and Grill and then margaritas at a Mexican restaurant—the name of which, at that point, everyone was too drunk to notice. And so it went until 4 A.M. Monday, when he and Amanda finally stumbled back to their two-bedroom apartment in Chelsea.

• • •

As Flight 93 stormed down the runway that Tuesday morning, Mark had to chuckle about the celebration that had ended only 29 hours earlier. As sloppy drunk as he and his friends were Monday morning, this was exactly why he had moved to New York nine months ago—to have as much unrelenting fun as possible in one of the few cities that could put his energy level to a test. The weekend would be one they would never forget, and thanks to the photographs he'd captured throughout the weekend with the disposable camera now packed in his duffel bag, it would be one he personally would be certain to remember. As the Boeing 757 finally lifted off the ground at 8:42 A.M., Mark more than likely gripped the sides of his seat and made a mental note to get the film developed after he landed in San Francisco.

"Hey, Mark. It's Ken. I am absolutely in shock right now. I just can't get over this. What's happening? I'm in Walnut Creek. Why don't you call me here.... But, my God, this is just devastating. I just can't believe this. Anyway, give me a call. Bye."

"Mark, this is your mom. It's 10:54 A.M. The news is that it's been hijacked by terrorists. They are planning to probably use the plane as a target to hit some site on the ground. So if you possibly can, try to overpower these guys if you can—'cause they will probably use the plane as a target. I would say go ahead and do everything you can to overpower them because they're hell-bent. You know the number here. OK, I love you, sweetie. Bye."

—the fourth and fifth unheard voice-mail messages left on Mark Bingham's mobile phone Sept. 11, 2001—the first from his friend Ken Montgomery and the second from his mother, Alice Hoglan

Mark was living the life his mother, Alice Hoglan, wished she had. At least that's what she always told him when she came for a visit, either during a layover in Manhattan or for a night on the town in San Francisco. Mark, who wanted both to show his mom a good time and to help her discover how much the cities had to offer, pulled out all the stops on these visits. During one of her more recent trips to New York he whisked her to the revolving restaurant at the top of the Marriott Marquis Hotel, where they admired the views of Times Square while sipping cocktails. Alice had to admit there was something uniquely spectacular about the bustling brilliance of the Great White Way when viewed from 49 floors up—even for a woman who makes her living 30,000 feet in the air. But in truth, none of the urban pizzazz mattered a whole lot to her. Alice just wanted to spend time with her son. The Broadway shows, the fine wines, and even the sandwiches from Carnegie Deli—so piled high with delicious meats she could hardly take a bite—were an added bonus that came along with the real prize, Mark.

In fact, if you asked her about it, Alice would tell you that she found cities a bit intimidating. And for this 52-year-old woman, who drives at least an hour in her brown half-ton pickup to get from her modest home in the Santa Cruz Mountains to work at San Francisco International Airport, that has probably always been the case.

The second of Herbert and Betty Hoglan's five children, Alice was born Oct. 3, 1949, in Toledo, Ohio. Describing her childhood, Alice first says that she comes from "Midwest stock" and that she was imbued with both "the Protestant work ethic and the pretty clear idea of the importance of people in your life." But when she really gets to reminiscing, it's clear that the real common denominator throughout her early years has been wanderlust. It's a characteristic this flight attendant clearly inherited from her parents and one she obviously passed on to her only child.

The Hoglan family approached life with a sense of optimism that far exceeded the standard American dream—even at its height during the "anything is possible" 1950s. So it makes sense that when Betty read *The Amazing Amazon*, a book published in 1952 by adventure writer Willard Price, she was more than swept away by its pages. She imagined her family among the South American orchards that Price described as bearing oranges "as big as footballs." A departure from Price's more standard adventure books for young adults such as *South Sea Adventure* and *Whale Adventure, The Amazing Amazon* was a firsthand account of his trek through interior Brazil and the vast and untapped resources available there. Describing one man's farm, Price wrote:

> There was a grove of mango trees, another of avocado trees, a field of banana plants, all heavily loaded with fruit. There was a tract of good pasture land covered with fresh green elephant grass. In the woods within the borders of Pero's property were fine hardwoods, mahogany, cedar, towering skyscrapers of trees loaded with Brazil nuts and cream nuts, and huge, wide-spreading fig and garlic trees. There were trees valuable for their oils very much in demand in the industrial

north. He had planted several acres to cocoa, and another tract to rubber.... The world needed Amazonia. Men who dared develop its riches were performing a great service.

And if that succulent description wasn't enough to catch the imagination of a young family eager to find its place in the world, Price followed it up with the real kicker: The Brazilian government was practically paying people to come down to cultivate its Amazon River regions.

Tens of thousands of pioneers are today flooding from the coastal cities back into the wilderness—or what was wilderness a few years ago, the watershed of Amazon tributaries, the rivers Tocantins, Araguaya, and Xingu. This movement is called by the government that has sponsored it the *March para o Oeste,* the March to the West.

This drive is heavily financed. Article 199 of the 1946 Constitution provides that during a period of twenty years three percent of national tax revenues shall be applied to the economic development of the Amazon region. Supplementing this federal appropriation, the states and territories of the region are required to contribute three percent of their income to the federal *Plano da Valarizcao da Amazonia* (Amazonian Development Plan).

That's not all. Municipalities in the area must allocate three percent of their revenues to the same project.

That was all Betty needed to coax Herbert to pack just about everything they owned into three giant shipping containers. Those containers were then loaded, along with the entire family, onto an ocean liner that went first to Liverpool, England—allowing the Hoglans to explore Europe for about three weeks—before steaming back across the Atlantic to Santos, Brazil. The plan was derailed, though, by a problem never considered in Price's prose—a clash between the penny-pinching Herbert and the money-hungry Brazilian government. "The Brazilian Customs wanted to charge Mom and Dad some outrageous sum as duty [for the three shipping containers]," Alice remembers. "Dad balked, hired an attorney, and that was a beginning of a 13-month wrangle during which time we lived on boxes and cots in a rented house in São Paulo." So much for living off the land.

As rough as the living was for the Hoglans south of the equator, Alice doesn't remember having anything other than the typical experiences of an 8-year-old girl. "I was in third grade, my teacher was Mrs. Levy, and I had a terrible crush on a blond boy named Landon, whose father was a corporate executive for some U.S. corporation," she says. "Sure, it was a real strange existence, but I felt very secure and loved, and that was what mattered to me at the time."

At the end of their 13-month unsuccessful fracas with the Brazil Customs department, the Hoglans returned to the United States in 1959. But things never really slowed down. Betty wanted to live in Florida, while Herbert preferred Southern California. And Alice remembers spending the remainder of her childhood moving back and forth between the two coasts. They also lived, for a brief time, in Fort Madison, Iowa—which was across the Mississippi River from Navoo, Ill., an early settlement of Mormon pioneers before they journeyed west to Utah after the murder of their founder, Joseph Smith, in 1844. While the family was in Fort Madison, Alice's oldest brother, Linden, first became acquainted with the Mormons and later became a member of the church himself. Through Linden's involvement in the church, Alice, when she was 15 and living in Miami, also became a congregant.

"As a 15-year-old, I was attracted to the stability of [the

Church of Jesus Christ of Latter-day Saints] and the message," Alice explains. "The LDS people feel that they have the true church and that their male leaders have the sole authority to speak for Christ. This was a powerful message for a 15-year-old searching for an answer." Hinting at what was probably another strong factor in her conversion, Alice adds, "I was also impressed by the personalities of the missionaries," referring to the pairs of young men the church has historically sent out to do apostatizing.

Apparently, church officials were impressed with Alice too, enough that they offered her a scholarship to attend the church-owned Brigham Young University in Provo, Utah. In addition for paying for part of her school, the scholarship was enough to give her still-money-conscious father a better opinion of the Mormon Church. "That was all my dad needed as an incentive to let me go," she says.

After 18-year-old Alice arrived in Provo, however, she started to feel different about the church and its teachings. "I began to bristle when I was exposed to some of the dogmatism I saw," she says. "Essentially, I began to question Joseph Smith's story and the veracity of the basic tenant of Mormonism—that it was the only church with the authority to speak for God." What didn't bother her at the time was the church's stand on an issue that has since gained significantly more importance in her life: equal rights. As women across the country campaigned for passage of the Equal Rights Amendment, Mormon Church leaders in Salt Lake City fervently urged the proposal's failure, calling the ERA "a moral issue with many disturbing ramifications for women and for the family as individual members of a whole." Church president Spencer Kimball said the ERA "would strike at the family, [which is] humankind's basic institution."

Homosexuality, meanwhile, was not an issue many Mormons discussed while Alice was at BYU. But university president Dallin H. Oaks made it clear in 1975 that drug users and homosexuals were "two influences we wish to exclude from the BYU community." Oaks was responding to an Associated Press story that had reported that university security officers were using electronic surveillance devices to investigate students who were suspected of being gay or lesbian.

"I never thought of myself as being particularly oppressed [as a woman], because I've always been a pretty powerful person," Alice says. "But I do remember there was some political event and the Relief Society [a Mormon women's group] president was speaking violently against women having equal rights, and it really surprised me. I guess I was pretty ignorant about the [church's] oppression of women at the time. And when it came to homosexuality, frankly, that was not a very important issue to me at the time."

Alice's eyes were opened a bit wider in the spring of 1969 when, after she finished her sophomore year at BYU, she decided to strike out on her own for the first time and "headed like a horse in a burning barn" to Santa Monica, Calif. Once in California, she immediately secured a job at Sambo's restaurant, where she had worked the previous summer in Miami Beach, and ran head first into her future—in the form of Jerry Bingham.

Jerry, a tall 26-year-old from Tucson, Ariz., who Alice remembers as being a "big, cute guy," was a Sambo's manager at the time. But his relationship with Alice was never bound by traditional boss-employee confines, he says. The two of them started dating almost immediately and quickly moved in with each other. "She needed a place to stay, and since we were working different hours anyway, I told her she could stay in my apartment," he says. And when Jerry was transferred to a Sambo's restaurant in Orange County, Calif., that summer, Alice followed. Then that fall, when she returned to BYU for her junior year, she learned she was pregnant.

The news was devastating to Alice, who as a Mormon, was

expected to live by the church's strict standard of chastity until marriage. "I was humiliated," she says. "But Jerry was very much the gentleman and was excited about the prospect of a child." The couple drove to Las Vegas, where they were married in one of the city's many wedding chapels, and then went their separate ways again—Alice back to Provo to finish out the semester and Jerry to Phoenix, where he readied himself and a home for his new family.

Twenty-year-old Alice had some reservations about becoming a mother, and she still had them when Mark was born on May 22, 1970. Named Gerald Kendall Bingham, or Jerry, he was a plump baby whose brown Shirley Temple-like curls grew as quickly as he put on weight. "He used to drink every bottle I gave him," Alice remembers. "And I, inexperienced mother that I was, didn't know I wasn't supposed to be feeding him every couple of hours. Then my Aunt Mary took a look at him one day and asked, 'Alice, how often are you feeding that baby?' She was flabbergasted when I told her six bottles a day. He was one chubby dude."

But even as Alice kept her baby's belly full of formula, she couldn't help think of the way things could have been for her and, as far as she was concerned, the way they should have been. "I resented being a young mother because it wasn't my plan," she says. "Clearly it was my fault, but it certainly was not my plan." The unexpected baby boy had a way of growing on his reluctant mother, though. "What happened, when [Jerry] was born is that I said, 'Oh, he's a beautiful little boy, and I love him. But I'm not going to like him when he's a year old.' And when he got to be a year old, I said, 'Oh, I still love him, but I'm not going to like him when he's 3.' And that's the way it went, and I ended up loving him his whole life."

No baby, however, could convince Alice to stick with her marriage. Within weeks of her son's birth, it became painfully obvious that she and Jerry Bingham had little in common—

other than baby Jerry. The Mormon Church was a major source of the couple's difficulties, as Jerry remembers. "I looked into [joining] the church, but I couldn't believe how anybody believed that way," he says. "But at that time, the church was a very integral part of Alice's life, and that was a big problem for us." For Alice, her reason for leaving was much simpler. "We really weren't cut out for the long haul," she says.

When baby Jerry was about 2 1/2 months old, Alice threw him under her arm "like a football" and bolted for the Phoenix airport, where the two caught the first flight to Miami and the comfort of the Hoglan home. "My life just felt as if it was in a bad spot, and I knew I had to take my baby and get out of there," she says. But what's important, she adds, is that the dramatic action she took that summer day in 1970 did more than get the two of them out of Phoenix—it also marked the beginning of what became a 31-year partnership between mother and son. "Mark and I became a real team. We were inseparable and we loved each other," she says. "And I don't think he ever doubted that he was the most important thing in my life."

After their arrival in Miami, Alice and her baby, whom she started to call Kerry—by taking the "K" from his middle name—were immediately welcomed back into her parents' hurly-burly home. With Linden and his new wife, Ruth, and Alice's younger brothers and sister, Lee, Vaughn, and Candy, still living under Herbert and Betty's roof, Alice and Kerry were hardly an added burden. In fact, the baby actually added a little levity to the household, which was already far from boring. Such was the case when Lee and Vaughn, in an act photographer William Wegman would have admired, put baby Kerry through a series of staged photo sessions. In one shot he was a blackjack shark, cards in his hand, a cigar stuffed in his mouth, and a green visor propped on his head. In another they set him next to the pool table and put a cue in his hand. "They treated him like a stuffed doll some of the time," Alice says. "And a baby thrives with that kind of attention."

As much comfort and familiarity living at home provided Alice, and as much attention it afforded her son, she knew it had to be temporary. Part of the reason she had gone to BYU in the first place—and a large part of the reason she went to work in Santa Monica at the end of her sophomore year—was to establish her independence apart from her family. Having a baby didn't change that desire. Sure, it complicated her plans, but it also stoked her desire with purpose.

With that purpose in mind, she returned to college—this time Florida Atlantic University—and in 1973 earned an education degree from the first graduating class of what by that time was renamed Florida International University. In addition to staying on top of her studies during this time, Alice held down a number of odd jobs—the oddest being a three-month stint as a bunny at Miami Beach's Playboy Plaza Hotel. It was quite a change for the former BYU coed to become a Playboy bunny. But for Alice, who had moved out of her parents' house by this point and was living with Kerry on a shared front porch in Miami Beach, it was way to put food on the table. "I remember I used to be really glad that they fed us [at the Playboy Plaza Hotel]," she says. "But you had to get into your costume before you ate because it was so tight. The lacing was so tight, in fact, that I used to lose the circulation in my hips."

At the same time, Alice was completing the student teacher requirement for her degree, sometimes forgetting to take off the false eyelashes and heavy makeup she was required to wear as a bunny before talking her post in front of her junior high school consumer education students. "Eventually I figured out that I needed to wear flats rather than spiky heels in order to be taken seriously," she says.

Upon graduating, she accepted a teaching position at Miami Springs High School. While the job offered Alice some of the stability she had been seeking, it was far from being the right fit. "As it turned out, I didn't like teaching at all," she says. "I loved the subject and I loved the kids, but I was only 24 and I was a terrible disciplinarian. The kids used to run roughshod over me, so I bailed after that first year."

Full-time job or not, things were still tight at home, which by this time was a houseboat docked on the Miami River, in the shadow of the Orange Bowl. But that didn't bother Kerry—by now a quiet and contemplative 4-year-old— because he didn't know any different. When his mother was home, he was happy to spend time with her. But he was equally happy when he had to keep himself occupied. He was thrilled when, at his grandparents' house, he could sneak away to his uncle's treasured aquarium, pull out a fish, and pet it. "Vaughn couldn't figure out why his fish kept dying," Alice remembers. And when Kerry was alone in his own living room he eventually learned to construct fantastical "air houses" by putting a box fan at one end of pinned-together bedsheets. "They were these huge billowing structures," Alice says. "And he would get in the middle, with the sheets flopping all around him, and just sit there cross-legged. It was a pretty cool thing."

In truth, it was Alice who was still struggling to bring the different sides of her single mother–working woman life in concert. And she often did so with comical finesse. After leaving Miami Springs High, Alice became a flight attendant for National Airlines—"I went from being a Playboy bunny to 'I'm Alice, fly me,'" she jokes, referring to the airline's pop- ular 1970s advertising campaign, which featured its flight attendants. She tried to schedule the shortest trips possible, ones that would require her to be gone from home only one or two nights at a time. And on those nights she would have Kerry stay with one of two reliable women she had lined up as baby-sitters.

One time, when Kerry was 6 years old, Alice had to take him with her on a trip. And, as luck would have it, the two of them found themselves on a flight where there was no room for Kerry. So the ever-resourceful Alice stowed her son away in one of the airplane's closets—an experience that was no doubt thrilling for the boy and, albeit stuffier, probably not too unlike the time he liked to spend in his air houses. "Oh, it wasn't a good idea, but it was only an hour-long or so flight," Alice says, laughing. "Flight attendants were passing him food in the closet." The closet flight turned out to be one of the most memorable trips for Kerry, who grew up to become a very frequent flyer. "He reminded me of it a couple years ago," Alice says. "And believe it or not, I had completely forgotten."

Soon after Alice and Kerry moved to Florida, Jerry followed. And even though the brief stab he and Alice took at patching up their relationship didn't hold, Jerry says he still saw his son whenever he could, taking him on trips or having him over for the weekend. "We had a lot of fun," he says. "But one of his visits stands out for me more than any of the others."

Jerry owned a restaurant in Boca Raton at the time and had 6-year-old Kerry and his stepsister Kelly staying at his apartment behind the business. "I had both of them sleeping on the bed, and it was cool that night, so I took a blanket and covered them up with it," Jerry says. "Then later, after I went to lay on the couch, they both got up, took the blanket off themselves, and came over to put it on me. I never forgot it."

The Hoglan family was on the move again in 1978—this time back to Southern California—and Alice and 8-year-old Kerry joined them in Riverside, where Kerry started third grade in September. The move was just the first in a series he and his mother made throughout California between 1978 and 1983, meaning that Kerry enrolled in five different schools in as many years.

As they would have on any child, the moves had a lasting impact on young Kerry. Most significantly, he grew accustomed to being the new kid in class. That must have helped lay the foundation for what friends would later say was one of his most admirable characteristics—his ability to make new friends no matter where he was.

Matt Hall, who describes himself as a shy guy who never used to make the first move when it came to introductions, remembers being amazed by Mark's ability to meet new people when they went to New Orleans over Labor Day in 2001. "He took me by the hand in front of the Phoenix bar and said, 'Let's go meet people,'" Hall says. "Then he started going up to people and saying, 'Hi, I'm Mark Bingham from California. This is Matt from New Jersey.'"

That's not to say Kerry had perfected his people skills when he was in elementary school. Alice remembers that her son was never at a loss for a pal to play with when he was young, but some of his most significant friendships at this time were of the four-legged and, sometimes, creepy-crawly variety. His fascination for animals extended back to when he was toddler, fumbling for the fish in his uncle's aquarium. And Alice didn't hesitate when it came to getting her son one of his first pets, a fish named William, when they were still in Florida. But along with the move to the West Coast came Kerry's requests for more exotic pets. First there was a rat named Mikey.

"We thought Mikey was a male. Then we got him a male 'friend' and learned almost immediately that Mikey was, in fact, female," Alice says. "Mikey had babies and then she had another set of babies. Then one morning [Kerry] came in and yelled, 'Mom, Mikey had babies again, and guess what? They're sucking on one of the babies.' So I had to explain to him that Mikey was now a grandmother and that this brood was, in fact, from one of her babies." Kerry ended up with 47 rats before most of them died as a result of an epidemic of some sort that Alice says swept through Mikey's family.

Then there was the pet king snake that Kerry carried with him wherever he went. At one point, Alice says the snake got loose in her Toyota Celica and hid behind the car's dashboard.

"For weeks I was driving around with a snake somewhere in the car," she says. "Then one day I came out from work and the snake was coiled in the front seat, evidently ready to go back to his master."

After Riverside, Kerry and his mother moved to nearby Redlands, where Kerry started fourth grade and made a decision that had a significant effect on the rest of his life. Over the previous few years he had become increasingly bothered by the fact that most of the other people who shared his first name were girls. So Alice offered her son an opportunity that few other people ever have, as they were walking to school for his first day in fourth grade. "I said, 'Kerry, you've been complaining about your name, and now's the time to change it, because people here don't know you yet.'" After thinking about his mom's proposition for just a minute, he responded, "OK, I'll be Mark."

"It was a brave and very definite thing. He just chose it," Alice remembers of that day. "And when we got to the classroom and the teacher said, 'This is Mark Bingham,' I heard a kid say, in a whining voice, 'Another Mark!'"

Even more significant, though, was another change that took place for Mark in his first few years in California—his transition from being a little boy wholly dependent on his mother to becoming a young man who accepted an increasing level of responsibility for his family's welfare. At no time was it more apparent that this transition had taken place than in the summer of 1980—when Alice, like her mother had been in the 1950s, was inspired by an author to make another move.

Actually, as Alice explains, the move was prompted by more than just a book. "I was briefly engaged to a very nice man when we were living in Redlands, and decided to bolt just before the wedding. So, in July 1980 we picked a place on the map, and I was a John Steinbeck fan, so we chose Monterey." Although he is best known for his epic chronicle of one family's struggles during the Great Depression, *The Grapes of Wrath*, Steinbeck's muse was his native Northern California. The cities of Salinas and Monterey were main characters in several of his novels. And even when describing one of these city's seedier sides, he did it in a way that made readers want to experience the slime and the grime of the place for themselves. "Cannery Row in Monterey in California is a poem, a stink, a grating noise, a quality of light, a tone, a habit, a nostalgia, a dream," he began his 1945 novel *Cannery Row*. "Cannery Row is the gathered and scattered, tin and iron and rust and splintered wood, chipped pavement and weedy lots and junk heaps, sardine canneries of corrugated iron, honky tonks, restaurants and whore houses, and little crowded groceries, and laboratories and flophouses."

For Alice, it sounded like as good a place as any for a fresh start. And she and Mark, who arrived at Monterey's Laguna Seca campground on July 4 with little more than the $19 she had in her pocket, needed just that. Monterey, though, wasn't the same place it had been in Steinbeck's day. Alice and Mark were essentially homeless for three weeks—living in the back of Alice's pickup—and it wasn't as easy for a couple of wanderers to live off the land as it had been in *Of Mice and Men*. But somehow they made it work. When Alice left the campground each morning in search of a job, Mark went down to the wharf—sometimes to wander and take in the same sights and sounds that had inspired Steinbeck, but often to throw a fishing line in the water in the hope of catching dinner for his mother and himself. "Mark sustained us," Alice says. "More than one occasion he and I would grill up and eat what he was able to provide for us that night."

Even after Alice found a job as a secretary and they moved out of the campground and into their own apartment, Mark continued providing for the family by selling Alice's baked goods throughout the neighborhood. "I look back on it now and say, 'Wow, that was a really cool, character-building experience,'" Alice says of those tough days in Monterey. "But it was pretty grim. There was never a lot of money, and that may have been the nadir of our existence."

"*Mark, apparently it's terrorists and they're hell-bent on crashing the aircraft. So if you can, try to take over the aircraft. [fumbling for words] There doesn't seem to be much plan to land the aircraft normally. So I guess your best bet would be to try to take it over, if you can. Or tell the other passengers. There's one flight that they say is headed toward San Francisco. It might be yours. So, if you can, group some people and perhaps do the best you can to get control of it. I love you, sweetie. Good luck. Bye-bye.*"

"*Hey, Mark, it's Todd. Can you give me a call and let me know that you're OK when you get a chance? I'm watching all this shit on the news. OK, bye.*"

"*Mark Bingham, it's Paul Eto. It's 8:15 West Coast time. Just saw all the news. Wanted to check how you're doing. Hope you're OK. I'm sure you'll call your mom and Kathy. Talk to you later. Bye.*"

—the sixth, seventh, and eighth unheard voice-mail messages left on Mark Bingham's mobile phone on Sept. 11, 2001—the first from his mother, Alice Hoglan; the second from his friend Todd Sarner; and the third from a family friend, Paul Eto

THREE

CALIFORNIA'S SANTA CRUZ MOUNTAINS are the one thing that, geographically at least, separate the Silicon Valley from coastal communities such as Santa Cruz and Aptos. Sometimes, when a rainstorm pushes in from the Pacific Ocean and soaks those towns that straddle it, the Santa Cruz Mountains are also the one thing that keeps the valley dry. Essentially, the clouds get stuck on the mountains, as if the wind forgot where it was pushing them, and the rain falls and falls on the tiny communities that dot Highway 17, which connects the valley to the coast.

April 30, 1983, was one of those days. And as Alice, Mark, and Mark's Aunt Candy moved into their new cabin in Redwood Estates, the rain came from two directions—both falling from the sky and gushing down the neighborhood's steep streets. "I remember Mark working really hard that day," Alice says. "He was only 12, and he was already bigger than both of us. So we really needed his help. But he was headstrong and feisty, and I'm sure he would have preferred to be doing anything else other than moving us into another home during such a rainstorm."

Indeed, in the five years since they had moved to California, he and his mother had moved at least five times. The move to Redwood Estates was a little different, however. The mountain community, which was first established as a cabin retreat for city folks in the 1930s, was affluent compared to the places they'd lived in Monterey and East San Jose. The cabin, which sat on one of the many bends toward the bottom of one the main roads through Redwood Estates, had two floors, so Mark could basically claim the basement as his own. "It was certainly a step up for us both," Alice says.

Several miles southwest of Los Gatos, Redwood Estates is considered part of the city, and students who live there and in the neighboring mountain communities are bused to schools in town. Mark was just three weeks shy of his 13th birthday on his first day as an 8th grader at R.J. Fisher Middle School. Classmate Damon Billian remembers seeing Mark that first day and, because he had been the "new kid" a few times himself, introduced himself. "I went up and asked him if he wanted to play football with us in the courtyard," Damon says. "And the poor guy. The first time he came out to play with us he ran into a pole while he was trying to catch a pass. He wasn't very good at sports at that point."

Even though Mark was already a huge fan of professional sports—especially Miami Dolphins football—he didn't hit the field very often himself. Already 5-foot-8 and, as his mother recalls, "a chubby baby who turned into an awkward, long-legged teenager," Mark much preferred exercising his mind by creating fantasy worlds in games such as Dungeons & Dragons to making a fool of himself on the practice field.

Damon didn't share Mark's interest in D&D, but the two nevertheless became fast friends. "He was just a cool, bright kid," he says. "And pretty soon I got rid of my other best friends to start hanging out with him." As any best friend would, Damon set out to teach the rather insecure Mark how to protect himself. "He had a mouth on him already," he explains. "And when people made fun of him he would talk back. But then when things started to get physical he didn't know what to do. I think part of it was because he didn't have a brother and didn't do the sibling rivalry kind of stuff.

"One time when we were in eighth grade there was this guy, who was about Mark's height but a lot heavier, who started picking on him. And since I was about a foot shorter than Mark, I think I kind of shocked him when I went up and said, 'Dude, don't take that from him! Just hit him like this,' and then I smacked the guy really hard."

Damon's lessons in hard knocks didn't stop there. He then set out to teach his new friend how to hit for himself. But rather than using a heavy bag, a speed bag, or any other traditional boxing aids, "we would just punch each other," Damon says, laughing. "And Mark got pretty good!"

In 1985 both Alice and Candy started working as flight attendants for United Airlines, which for Mark and his friends meant they could have the run of the whole cabin on the nights that Mark's mother and aunt were away on trips. "Mark actually spent a lot of time with me at my place, having dinner with my family and stuff," says Damon, who also lived in the Santa Cruz Mountains. "But we also spent a lot of after-school time at his place when his mom was away working." On one such occasion, when he and Mark were both 15, Damon remembers they found a collection of the small bottles of alcohol that are served on airplanes, "and we just started opening them, mixing them all together, and then drinking them. Then Mark started calling everybody in the Los Gatos phone book and saying that I was going to kick their ass," he says. "I think that was both the first time either one of us got drunk and the first time we ended up throwing up from drinking."

By the time Damon and Mark were sophomores at Los Gatos High School they had welcomed fellow sophomore Todd Sarner into their fold, and within a year Cameron Dawson, who was a year older, was also a part of the group. "I think what brought us together originally is that we didn't fit into any of the cliques," Todd says. "We weren't really jocks, and we weren't really the nerdy, brainy kids either. We kind of got along with everyone but didn't identify enough with any of them to become part of their group." So the boys often did their own thing.

Whether all together or in various combinations of the four, they started to consider Mark's cabin the headquarters for their high jinks. Sometimes they would collaborate on music videos—complete with big hair, makeup, and air guitar—that paid tribute to some of their favorite heavy metal bands, including Kiss, Iron Maiden, Metallica, and Mark's favorite band at the time, Queensryche. "They would get made up in these outrageous getups—I think Kiss was one of the worst—and they used my makeup to do it," Alice says, admitting that she didn't quite understand her son's attraction to the music. "I'd see the videotapes they made, and Mark would have this fierce, really angry look on his face and he'd be punishing this broom that was supposed to be his guitar. I guess it was just part of the growing-up process."

One time, Alice came home and found that Mark and some of his friends had painted the word "Satan" on the concrete floor in a part of the cabin that was being remodeled. "As soon as they painted it I think Mark got afraid of what I was going to say, so he tried to change it to read 'Saturday' instead. And I was like, 'What's this? Saturday?'"

Not all of their video projects had to do with the dark side, though. Mark used the video camera for some of his school-work too. For example, for a physics class he produced a video called *The San Anton Massacre II*. The plot revolved around Cameron, who was going to go around Redwood Estates killing Mark's friends by using the laws of physics. "For example, he was supposed to use refracted light to kill me," Todd says. "So I was sitting there reading a book while Cameron put a magnifying glass above my head. Then off-camera someone lit a cigarette and positioned it so it looked like there was smoke coming off of my head."

The video's thrilling finish was supposed to be Mark's murder by momentum. Mark had Cameron and Todd get in Cameron's car—which was a "big, old American car," as Todd remembers—and instructed Todd to videotape from the backseat as Cameron drove the car after Mark, who was going to be running down the street. "But he didn't tell us how the scene was going to end," Todd says. "So we were driving down the hill at about 20 miles an hour while Mark ran and screamed, 'Oh, my God! Oh, my God!' Then all of a sudden he jumped on the hood—not only denting it, but totally smashing out the front windshield. I kept taping for a couple seconds, but then I got worried if Mark was OK. So I turned it off. And rather than telling us if he was all right, he immediately yelled, 'Todd, why did you turn off the damn camera?'"

Today, when Alice hears stories like this and others about things that took place at her cabin when she was away at work, she shakes her head and smiles, with both amazement and regret. "I was distracted a bit during the time my son was growing up. I was focused on my own shallow and petty affairs, and I let a lot of important things about my son go by without giving them the thought that they deserved," she acknowledges. "But my memory of Mark is that he always seemed to be unfolding as he should, and he seemed to be on a good track. His friends were exemplary, and his pursuits—the things that he was focused on—seemed full of merit and suitable for him. I can't say that I ever really worried about him. I may have been distracted, but I was always his mom, and I don't think he ever wanted for love."

One day during Mark's sophomore year, when he was riding the bus home from school, his focus was on nothing but the pretty, long-brown-haired girl sitting in front of him. "There wasn't enough room for me to sit by the time I got on the bus, so I sat on the stair in the back, and my head was right next to Mark's knee," says Malaina Taylor. "When my head brushed against him one time, he said, 'Oh, you have really soft hair.'" Just a freshman at the time, Malaina says she immediately felt the blood rush of a blush. And even though he saw how red-faced she was, he continued. "You know why I said that, don't you?" he asked. "Because I was told guys are supposed to say those sort of things to girls." The two of them flirted the remainder of the ride home, and by the time the bus reached Mark's stop he had Malaina's phone number in his hand. "He called me that night," she says. "I was so excited."

Mark and Malaina became a couple right away. He sometimes went to her house for dinner when Alice was at work, and Malaina sometimes brought meals to Mark's house when his mother was away. "He was the perfect boyfriend," she says. "He would even come to my diving meets—and usually was the only person to show up."

But the romance quickly took on a pall of "boy meets girl but boy doesn't like girl as much as girl likes boy," Malaina says. "He told me, 'Mali, I can't date you anymore because you're too good for me.' And I said, 'That's not true, you're perfect.'" A long time would pass before Malaina understood why Mark broke things off so quickly.

Still, the two of them stayed as close as ever after they stopped dating. And when Malaina's family's house burned down during a forest fire in 1985, her mother paid Mark $5 an hour to help with the cleanup and reconstruction. It was then, Malaina says, that she knew she and Mark would always be friends. "He asked me for my Social Security number," she remembers. "And when I asked what he wanted it for, he said, 'Because I want to be able to get a hold of you no matter where you go on this planet.'"

. . .

It was as a student at Los Gatos High that Mark had what most of his friends and family agree was one of the most significant encounters of his life—with the sport of rugby football. A sport that got its start in England in the early 1800s, rugby is tremendously popular in the British Commonwealth countries as well as France and South Africa. But it has never attracted as much attention in the United States. So no one knows for certain where Mark, a tremendous football fan who ran into poles when he actually tried to play the game, got the idea to try out for rugby. "I imagine he just saw a sign and decided to check it out with a number of his friends," says Delman Smith, the high school team's coach, who was nevertheless very pleased that Mark showed up that day. "His size is what made him stand out right away. He was real tall, and that was helpful," he says. "That and the fact that he hadn't been spoiled by American football. Many guys learn skills in football that are counterproductive to rugby. But Mark was a clean slate, and he took to the game right away."

A rugby team, which is made up of 15 players, includes eight forwards and seven backs. The backs tend to be the faster players, who handle the ball, which is fatter and rounder than a football. The forwards, meanwhile, are the bigger, more aggressive players, who are responsible for directing the forward plays of the game. Mark played position number eight, which, according to Delman Smith, is the key position for the forwards.

Unlike in American football, rugby players are not allowed to throw the ball forward. They can only throw it sideways or backwards. Any forward movement on the field is initiated by kicking or dribbling the ball or, as is most common, constant combinations of tossing and running with it. While rugby, like football, involves a lot of physical contact, rugby players wear no protective clothing or pads. And rugby allows for very few player substitutions, which means that once players are put on the field they usually play the entire game. Rugby also allows for no time-outs during a game's two 40-minute play periods. As a result, team members are required to make split-second decisions about strategy despite extreme cardiovascular fatigue and constant physical confrontation. More than many other sports, rugby is a battle of will.

For some reason this game was a perfect fit for a guy who, hardly more than a year ago, had his best friend teaching him how to stand up for himself. "I think rugby is just where Mark physically found himself. His way of being just clicked with the sport," Todd says. "He knew he was going to get hurt—and he got hurt all the time—but he didn't care. His safety wasn't a priority. After he started playing rugby he treated everything he wanted in life like that ball. He would just say to himself, *There's the ball. I'm going to get it, no matter what comes between it and me.*"

That attitude convinced Coach Smith to appoint Mark as team captain for two consecutive seasons—the first and only time that ever happened at Los Gatos. The captain is a very important position in rugby, Smith explains, because the coach is not allowed any contact with the players during the game, so all direction must come from the captain.

His fearless approach also caused Mark, whose body became riddled with scars, a lot of injuries during high school—including a broken arm, a couple broken noses, and a lot of bleeding. In fact, Coach Smith says Mark suffered more serious injuries over the years than anyone else he can remember. However, he adds, "I think it was more a case of bad luck than it was viciousness on the field."

Bad luck or not, the rough-and-tumble aspect of the game made it hard to watch for Alice, who usually spent all of the match's 80 minutes wincing on the sidelines. "I would go to the game and just wring my hands and *ugh*," she says, pretending to shiver. "Mark would usually be in the middle of these scrums, and he had to do a lot of fierce things. There would also be a lot of cussing and bloody sweat flying around." Nevertheless, she adds, it was Mark's experience on the Los Gatos rugby club that transformed him from gangly teenager into a confident young man. "I remember Mark looking back on those days and telling me that he felt such a strong pressure to perform in high school," she says. "When he gravitated to rugby he said he didn't feel that pressure any longer."

Rugby also afforded Mark his first chance to travel out of the country—on two tours with the Los Gatos rugby club and a third with the Northern California all-star team. It was on one of the tours with the Los Gatos team, to Canada, that Mark broke his arm. "It was a displaced fracture of the forearm," Coach Smith says. "But the doctors straightened it out and he insisted on staying with us the whole tour."

He was injured again on the team's second trip, this time to Fiji and New Zealand, but it didn't happen on the field. Many stories involving Mark differ depending on who is telling them, and that is especially so in this case. According to Todd Sarner, Mark was trying to catch a flight home from Auckland. Because he was flying on his mother's employee pass he wasn't with the rest of the team members, who had already left for the States. "He kept getting bumped, and I think he ended up staying at the airport for a whole day," Todd says. "Well, he eventually ended up in the airport bar, since the drinking age in New Zealand was 18, and the next time he got bumped from the flight I think he started to pee right there to show his displeasure." At that point, Todd says, airport security started to chase Mark, who ended up running through a plate-glass window, which resulted in an L-shaped gash on his leg.

Some time after that, Coach Smith and Mark's mother ran into each other. After talking for a while about the trip, including the fact that the Los Gatos team ended up in a tie with one of the top high school teams in New Zealand—a huge feat for U.S. ruggers—Alice said, "Mark sure made a mess on that farm, didn't he?" When the coach asked Alice what she was talking about, she said, "You know, when Mark and his friends got caught by the Fijian farmer with a machete as they were trying to steal sugar cane from his field." Coach Smith just shook his head, said, "You can't be serious," and then told Alice what had really happened. "I don't want to know any more about that!" Alice says today, laughingly. "Apparently, Mark was actually banned from the country for a while."

The all-star trip to Australia, which was part of that country's bicentennial celebration in 1988, certainly wasn't as eventful as Mark's time in New Zealand. And the squad did n't do nearly as well as the Los Gatos team had. Still, the trip stood out among the others because of the lifelong friendships he made when he was there. As was the case on all of these trips, Mark and his teammates were assigned billets when they arrived in the host country. In Sydney, however, no one was interested in hosting the team from the United States because, as Amanda Mark remembers, it was expected to be one of the worst of the visiting teams. "So a couple days before they were due to arrive our economics teacher, who was coordinator of our regional rugby events, pleaded with us to host some of the U.S. team members." Even though the tournament coincided with their high school certificate exam, Amanda, her friend Cathi Farnham, and two other girls agreed to help their teacher out. Mark ended up staying at Cathi's house but spent a lot of time with Amanda as well, as the four girls shirked a lot of their study time in order to show the rowdier side of Sydney to their guests from the U.S. "They were just a typical rugby union team," Amanda says. "The 26 of them were drinking, running around, going to strip clubs, and otherwise misbehaving. And the four of us girls kept right up with them."

One of the stops that week was a gay bar in Sydney's Darlinghurst-Paddington neighborhood, called the Exchange. "We used to go there every weekend because they played really, really good dance music," Amanda says, adding that she figured a gay bar wouldn't be too out there for a group of guys from the San Francisco area. She figured wrong, though. "They were all freaking out, including Mark. I think it was the first gay bar he had ever been to," she says. Mark clutched Cathi on one side of him and Amanda on the other and "just stared," Amanda says. "The funniest thing that night, however, happened when this absolutely beautiful woman went to the bathroom straight after Mark. A few minutes later he came running out and said, 'She just pissed standing next to me!' "

Mark kept up a correspondence with Amanda and Cathi and later became especially good friends with Amanda when she started making regular and extended trips to the United States after her graduation from high school.

As Mark neared the end of his own senior year he decided he wanted to attend the University of California, Berkeley. But after his application to the Cal system was processed he found that he had been placed at the Riverside campus in Southern California rather than at Berkeley. "When he told me about this, I told him I thought I could help," says Coach Smith. "So I got on the phone and called [Berkeley rugby coach] Jack Clark and said, 'Jack, I've got a kid here who can help your team. He's about 6-foot-4 and he's captain of my team.' And that was all I had to say. Jack was on the phone right away with Alice, and Mark was in."

But there was one final rite of passage before Mark's graduation from Los Gatos High and move to Berkeley: his senior prom. He asked Malaina, who then was living three hours north in Sonora, Calif., to be his date for the dance, and she agreed—even though, she remembers today, that her boyfriend wasn't thrilled with the idea. But if the start of Mark and Malaina's date was any indicator of how the rest of the night would progress, Malaina's boyfriend had nothing to worry about. "We got in the car to go to the dance and Mark said, 'I'm sorry, I'm really uncomfortable right now. I burned my ass on the fire last night,'" Malaina says.

The night before the dance, Mark and his friends had caravanned to a beach near Santa Cruz called Bonnie Doon and drank the night away by the light of a bonfire. And, as Cameron remembers, every time they threw a new log on the fire, they dared each other to jump on the flames. After Mark and a few others did so, the dare was notched up to jumping up and dancing on the fire. Again, Mark and a few others met the challenge. Not wanting to be outdone, Mark, who had gotten pretty drunk by this point, finally jumped on the fire, danced, and then sat down on it for a second. Later that night, "we scooped him into the car and he passed out," Cameron says. "A couple miles down the road my girlfriend and I noticed a horrific odor. It was really nasty and seemed to be coming from the backseat. When she turned to take a closer look at him, she saw that his shoes were totally melted, his jeans were singed on the edges, and most of his body hair—including his eyebrows— was curled and burned."

That next night at the prom, a hungover and singed Mark walked around like "he had a stick up his butt or something," Malaina says. "He wasn't Mr. Perfect Dancer, but we ended up staying on the dance floor all night. In fact, I don't think we ever sat down. I don't think he *could* sit down."

"Hey, it's Todd. Just give me a call when you get a chance. Sorry to call again, but I'm a little freaked out watching all this stuff. And I know... [pause] Well, anyway, just give me a call when you can. Bye."

"Mark, it's Jim. I'm trying to get a hold of you everywhere. Thanks."

"Hi, Mark. This is Judy calling. This is Tuesday, Pacific time, quarter to 10 in the morning, and Peer-Olaf and I are worried about you.... There are a lot of conflicting reports about flying and things like this and we just want to know where you are. Please give us a call. Thanks."

—the ninth, 10th, and 11th unheard voice-mail messages left on Mark Bingham's mobile phone on Sept. 11, 2001— the first from his friend Todd Sarner, the second from an acquaintance named Jim, and the third from his colleague Judy Curtis.

FOUR

IF ANY UNIVERSITY IS KNOWN FOR ITS radical student body, it's the University of California, Berkeley. Just consider a few of the school's most notable undergraduates: There was Julia "the Bubble Lady" Vinograd, who blew bubbles at the police during the 1969 riots in People's Park. Then there was Patty Hearst, who was studying history at Cal-Berkeley when the Symbionese Liberation Army kidnapped her in 1974. And who can forget Andrew "the Naked Guy" Martinez, who made headlines across the country in 1993 by refusing to wear to class anything more than his flip-flops and a smile?

Even at a school with such a colorful cast of characters, Mark Bingham stood out. This was especially so on Sept. 23, 1989. It was a Saturday afternoon and the first home football game of the season, and for Mark, who had started as a student at the school's extension program the previous fall in order to gain full-time admission to the popular school, it was his first home game as an official student.

As with most home openers, Memorial Stadium was packed with rowdy fans decked out in the traditional Golden Bear blue and gold. And the anticipation for the coming season was so intense that when Mark took his seat he couldn't tell if the tingle he felt crawl up his spine was pure excitement or the vibration created by the roar of the crowd when the marching band stuck up the "Big C" fight song.

Then again, Mark knew—along with his Chi Psi fraternity brothers crowded around him—that the shiver up his spine was just as likely from the alcohol he and the others had sneaked into the stadium and were now consuming with varying degrees of stealth. Mark had just pledged the fraternity the previous semester. And if he had been asked, or if he had bothered to think about it, he would have attributed part of his inebriation that afternoon to the simple fact that it's what new fraternity brothers do—impress others with the sheer volume of alcohol they can drink. Who needed an excuse, though? It was the first home game of the season. What better reason was there to get down-and-out blasted?

So Mark was definitely in good spirits when his Bears took the field against the Wisconsin Badgers. Possibly too good of spirits, as Chi Psi pledge Dave Kupiecki remembers. "He kept calling the Wisconsin team the Beavers" rather than the Badgers, he says. And when an older fraternity member suggested that his brothers hit the visitor section and harass the Wisconsin fans, Mark not only agreed but also one-upped him on the proposition. "Let's go get the Beaver!" he screamed, referring to the visiting team's mascot. "When Mark said, 'Come on guys, let's go,' our whole pledge class followed him, as if he were the Pied Piper," Dave says.

Not surprisingly, the blue-and-gold-clad invaders caught authorities' attention as they snaked their way into the otherwise Wisconsin-red visitor section. Enough attention that when they reached the wall that divides the stands from the playing field, the rabble-rousers were met by a phalanx of security guards. It appeared as though the brothers' plan to get the Badger was foiled before they laid their first trap. "We looked down on the field and were like, 'OK, they got us. We can't do it now,' Dave says. But Mark, who Dave remembers "got a crazy, kind of desperate look in his eyes" as the security guards approached, had a different reaction. "Without saying a word to anyone, he leaped over the wall and jumped onto the field."

As tens of thousands of fellow Cal fans looked on, Mark knocked the first security guard to the ground and did the same to the second who approached him. "It was like an open-field run in football," Dave says. "One guy finally tackled him, and Mark just dragged him along with his knee. Then another guy came in, grabbed Mark, and slowed him down some more. Finally, as about seven guards converged and slammed his body to the ground, Mark stretched out his arm—and his palm was about two feet from the Badger's foot."

Cal-Berkeley had another character to claim as its own, and the stadium erupted in an enormous cheer as Mark "the guy who tried to tackle the Badger" Bingham was taken to the city lock-up. He didn't get to see the Bears win the game by one touchdown, 20-14, but he certainly made his mark on everyone who did.

Saying he wanted to learn how people worked and how they interacted with one another, Mark declared psychology as his major. But friends say it was always clear that Mark's focus was more on the practical experiences college life offered than the academic ones, and he soon lost interest in lectures on mental processes and the inner mechanism of human motivation. According to Jeff Staiman, his fraternity brother and room-mate at the time, Mark found the personal relevance of his course load to be fairly abstract. "I remember one morning when I tried to get Mark to study for an astronomy exam—or at least to get up and attend [class]," Jeff says. "I didn't have much success."

His social life, however, seemed much more relevant, and "the Lodge," as the Cal Chi Psi members call their fraternity house, quickly became the center of his Berkeley universe. Not to say that the physical structure itself, which is located at 2311 Piedmont Ave., was much to speak of. From the outside, the Lodge is very much a stereotypical fraternity house. The front porch is lined with chipped, white-painted pillars and, as you might expect of a fraternity house in California, the front yard has been converted into a sand volleyball court. The place isn't any more unique inside either, as the basement bar (which bragged an always-on-tap keg when Mark lived there) proves.

Jeff remembers that he and Mark shared what most people would consider a pretty typical living environment for a fraternity. "We lived in a room with dirty plates and cups, laundry everywhere, papers and CDs on the floor—which we never vacuumed because we could never see it," he says. "Mark would have called it 'heinous.' And yet in this array of foulness, his bath towel stands out as particularly rank, a beacon of nausea."

As is the case with many fraternities, the Lodge abounded with Animal House-like experiences. There were the biannual Winnebago trips to Los Angeles for the Cal-UCLA football game. And of course there were the girls, some of whom, as legend has it, spent more nights with alternating men in the Lodge than they did at their own homes. Few of these stories, though, got as close to the realm of remarkable as those about the fraternity's annual luau. "It was huge," says Amanda Mark, who visited Mark many times at the Lodge and who flew from London to San Francisco in April 1993 in order to attend the fraternity's two-day luau. "The house was covered in turf on the floor, palm fronds on the wall, and tropical flowers on the roof." Fraternity members created a waterfall that cascaded down the main stairway—and another that fell from the top of the building into a pool in the backyard—to add to the experience.

Mark, who could be counted on to fire up just about any party, went the extra mile for the luau. In 1992, he used a volleyball net to help Todd Sarner, another frequent Lodge visitor, and several fraternity brothers surreptitiously scoop ducks up from a campus pond and place them in the fraternity's backyard. And while Mark was able to catch the ducks the following year, Amanda remembers that he still made a scene by the back pond. "Someone dared him to eat the goldfish," she says. "And I think he ate about three of them."

Chi Psi's Delta Delta chapter may have stood out from the others on campus because of the sheer amount of partying its members did, but Dave Kupiecki says it was the diversity of those members that really set the Lodge apart. "When most people think fraternity, they think of a bunch of guys who are 6-foot-tall, white, and wearing athletic gear. But we had 5-foot-4 Filipino guys, Hispanic guys, black guys, and white guys," Dave says. "There are fraternities that are vanilla, and I think Mark and I could have both gotten into those house. But that wasn't what we were drawn to."

A 6-foot-4 white guy who played on an athletic team, Mark had his own way of contributing to the diversity of the house, through the conversations he had with others. "In a predominately male situation like a fraternity, most conversation tends to be about female conquests, partying, or sports," Dave says. "But one of the big reasons people around the fraternity liked Mark was that you could just be sitting there talking to him about life, and about what was going on in the world, and about the fact that we were 22 and in college—and what does this all mean? He could stimulate those kinds of conversations, and he was genuinely interested in knowing what you thought."

What Dave and the other Chi Psi members didn't know at the time was just how much Mark's presence added to the fraternity's diversity factor. One of the reasons his conversations were composed of more than the standard girl-conquest dribble was that he wasn't as interested in those kinds of conquests.

Mark had known most of his life that he was different than the guys around him. He realized when he was 12 that the source of that difference was his sexual orientation—that he was gay. And as is the case for many young men and women when they learn they are gay, the realization confused him. After all, he had always loved sports and wasn't the least bit interested in dressing or acting in an effeminate manner (unless you count Halloween or the times he and his Aunt Candy sang "Don't Cry for Me, Argentina" at the top of their lungs). How could he be gay? It frightened him too because he couldn't help but worry about how his mother would react if she learned about it. The best bet, he figured, was to make sure no one ever found out.

Mark wasn't so convinced of his homosexuality that he didn't make several valiant attempts at heterosexuality. Dating women, he surmised, served several purposes: First, there was the possibility that if he dated women long enough he might learn to be attracted to them and, therefore, grow out of his homosexuality. And second, if he couldn't "cure" himself of his attraction to men, he could at least keep his fraternity brothers, family members, and friends from guessing he was gay by assuring they knew he dated women.

One of the women he dated was Stephanie Stark, a fellow Cal student who was a good friend to many of the guys at the Lodge. "Stephanie was one of those girls who knew she could come over and party with us—or just hang out in one of our rooms—and that nobody was going to hit on her. No drunken guys were going to do something to her," Dave says. "Eventually, it was obvious that a relationship was developing between Mark and Stephanie. And here it was, one of the closest girls to all the fraternity and one of the most beloved guys in the fraternity were developing a relationship. Everybody was rooting for them. It was like, 'Yeah!' "

The brothers were so excited by the possibility of the relationship that they didn't spend too much time scrutinizing its more intimate details. "I don't know if it was sexual in nature," Dave says. "But they were together for at least a couple of months. And every time there was a group event they would gravitate toward one another until the end of the night, when they were undoubtedly sitting next to each other. There was definitely something going on between Mark and Stephanie."

A freshman sociology major from nearby San Leandro,

Calif., Stephanie met Mark during "Welcome Week" 1990, when she and a friend whom she and Dave had in common stopped by the Lodge. She and Mark started dating three weeks later. "I think Mark told Dave that he liked me, and Dave told me," Stephanie says. "I was immediately drawn to him as well. He was the kind of guy who walked through a room and immediately brightened it up. Being with him was like being with a big whirlwind of fun."

The romantic part of their relationship lasted only about a month, by Stephanie's estimation. ("We realized pretty early on that we were just supposed to be good friends," she says.) And the time they spent together usually revolved around evenings of hanging out in her dorm room or pickup parties at the frat house. One of those nights that month, however, still stands out as one of Stephanie's favorites. Mark had asked her to be his date for Chi Psi's fall formal dance, and she was thrilled to have been asked. But as the date of the dance approached, Mark realized he had a family commitment that would keep him from joining Stephanie at the mixer held at the Lodge beforehand. He would have to meet her when she and the couples boarded the bus to head to the actual dance. "He was mortified that he wasn't going to be at the party," she says. "But I was friends with the guys in the house by this point and I told him not to worry about it." Mark did worry, though, and he did his best to make sure the night was as special as it was supposed to be, by making arrangements with a fraternity brother to buy Stephanie flowers for the mixer.

"So I got there and one of Mark's friends said, 'I have something for you from Mark,' and then he handed me a potted plant. 'Mark wanted me to get you flowers,' he said, 'but I thought a plant would last longer.' " A dutiful date, to be sure, Stephanie carried the plant throughout the party, only setting it down when it was time to board the bus. "When we got on the bus, Mark, who was wearing a suit and looked adorable, ran up and asked me where my flowers were." His face fell when he learned what happened. "He then went to the front of the bus, got on the loudspeaker, and said, 'I just want to apologize to my date. I want to say I'm sorry she got a potted plant instead of roses. I also want to apologize to her for being late and to tell her that I'm so excited to be with her tonight.' "

When friends fished for more details about his relationship with Stephanie, Mark just brushed them off, Dave says. And the few times where it was obvious to his brothers that Mark had scored with a girl, there was something different about his morning-after bragging. "He would be jovial about it, but he didn't have the typical swagger you might expect from a 20-year-old in college," Dave says. "He seemed too sensitive for that."

It was this more sensitive side of Mark that had, in part, attracted Dave to the Lodge in the first place. As a freshman from Minnesota, he initially felt out of place in Berkeley, both because he was from the Midwest and because it felt like he was the only one who didn't know anyone on campus—since the student body is made up primarily of Californians. "When I got to Cal and went through [Greek] rush a lot of people looked at me funny because of my style and just kind of blew me off," he says, adding that his mullet haircut may have helped distinguish him from the others on campus. When Dave got to the Lodge, he says, Mark "was just totally outgoing and jumped all over me right away. He wanted to know what I liked to do for fun, what kind of music I was into. He was just this big, goofy guy who was instantly friendly."

It's very likely that Dave's mullet was what caught Mark's attention—since he was used to being periodically ribbed by friends for his own out-of-control "short on the sides, long in the back" locks. But Mark and Dave had more in common than an outdated hairstyle. Dave was also an athlete—soccer, in his case. And the Minnesotan, who was a tad intimidated by the impending tryouts for the varsity team, was inspired by his new friend. Tall and lanky Mark looked more likely to fall down a flight of stairs than score points on the playing field. "The majority of the guys on the soccer team were making me look silly," Dave says. "Then I saw Mark, who when he played volleyball and stuff, wasn't very smooth and didn't look very athletic. I remember thinking, *This guy is supposed to be on one of the top-ranked rugby teams in the country?* It made me feel a ton better about my own standing on the soccer team."

That was before Dave actually saw Mark play rugby. "Oh my God, it was like he was made for the sport. All the things about him that I thought didn't fit into an athlete—I hadn't judged how that translated for rugby," he says. "Mark wasn't at this extreme level of cardiovascular health. I mean, he wasn't somebody who could go for a 12-mile run. But when he got on the rugby field, he just didn't stop. It was go, go, go, go, go, and then he kept going. It was astounding. And I knew right away that he was one of the guys on that team who really made a difference."

Actually, Mark wasn't one of the stand-out players his first rugby season, according to Cal's rugby coach Jack Clark. There were about 100 guys in the program then and, as Coach Clark remembers, Mark was a rank-and-file member of the squad. He became more of a presence, however, by 1991, when he proved his worth on the field and made the team's travel squad. "He was one of those guys that had versatility. He could play a tight forward position and he could play a back-row forward, and he would have gotten a lot of time in all of those positions," Clark says. "For a lot of guys, their physicality is all that they bring to the table, but Mark had good rugby instincts and he made good decisions. We would have gotten good rugby out of Mark no matter where we put him on the field." That year Mark first made the traveling squad the Cal rugby won the national collegiate championship, kick-starting a streak for the team that has lasted 12 years so far.

Despite Mark's success on the rugby field and in the Greek social scene, Cal is academically one of the toughest public institutions in the country. Nothing else mattered if Mark couldn't cut it in the classroom. And after his first year and a half on campus, Mark took a semester off to attend West Valley Community College in Saratoga, Calif., in an effort to bring up his sagging grade point average. He also took the semester to explore his sexuality away from the scrutiny of his fraternity brothers.

It was February 1990 when Mark picked up a copy of San Jose's *Metro* newspaper and, undoubtedly stricken with a serious case of butterflies, read a personal ad placed in the gay section by a 38-year-old man who called himself Frank. The ad read: "Discreet, GWM, seeking curious inexperienced 18-28 guys looking for a safe, gentle way to explore 'those feelings.' Relax! I felt the same way. Frank."

At the tail end of his teenage years by this point, Mark had spent nearly eight keeping the secret of his sexual orientation to himself. So when he sat down to write a letter in response to Frank's ad, the words rushed onto the paper. It was as if he were squeezing toothpaste from a fresh tube by clenching his grip on its middle. As good as it felt to be sharing his story—especially with someone he might never even meet—there was still the gnawing feeling that he would be better off if he just stayed the course, kept his secret, and continued to roll the tube from the bottom as he always had been taught.

2/2/90
10 P.M.

Dear Frank:

For me to write this letter was really tough. My fear of being discovered, exposed, or whatever is really strong, so I'm putting my full trust in you. Anyway, my name is Mark and I'm 19 years old. You sound like a really nice guy although I have no idea of your age or anything. Right now I'm taking 9 units at West Valley and I'm working. I'm a psychology major and I've got no idea what I want to do with my life, but I know I'll be a success at something. The thing that's been eating me up is that since I was like 12 I've known that I was gay. It never bugged me or made me feel guilty like many others, though. I messed around w/ other kids when I was young and I fantasized about sleeping with older guys a lot. I grew up and matured (and continue to mature) in a world where we see people dying of AIDS on TV. The stigma that goes with it not to mention the decomposing of the body itself that goes with this disease has kept me in mortal fear of touching another man (and most women). I'm not especially interested in women although I like most of them as friends. As a near-adult (17) I had one series of low-risk encounters w/ another guy at my school. I figured they were low risk because we were both pretty virginal. Now I'm missing something. I'm not a sex shark. I wouldn't enjoy sex w/ someone I didn't like. I really need to talk to someone who knows how I feel. I don't believe I could ever explore everything sexually with somebody I knew was questionable. [And] that is everyone these days. You could be AIDS-negative for three years and not develop antibodies or anything. It scares and angers me because I want to wake up in the morning next to another man.... My fantasy is to move away with my best friend/lover and live like Grizzly Adams in the forest. Hunting, planting, and playing in the daytime and cuddling on a bearskin rug with my partner by the fireplace at night. I know I'm just babbling and I probably sound like a basket case as well.

I'm a typical post-adolescent guy. I wish I was a kid again. I can't drink legally, and I'm too old to get into the movies for cheap. I couldn't wait to be older and now that that's happened I want to go back.

Freud would say that because my Mom was a single parent that's why I need a father figure type. I do want someone to confide in, but I don't really know who to talk to. Your ad really caught my eye.

I've never ever spilled my guts like this so I trust you'll use the utmost discretion and care. Through it all I'm a well-rounded guy. I'm happy with myself and my situation (but I'm vaguely horny all the time). I play sports and work hard and play hard. I'll pound beers when I don't have other obligations. I've always been a little contemptuous of real effeminate gays. I've had close friends for years that have no idea of my homo-sexuality and they won't find out. My mother and fam-ily will remain ignorant as well because no matter how much explaining I did it couldn't be the same relation-ship that I have now. I feel like an idiot telling you my life story—oh well. Write me a letter and tell me about yourself. Do you like pornos? How did you figure out that you were gay? How many guys have you made love with? Where is your secret freckle? Haha (Joke from SNL!)

2/2/90
11:59 P.M.

P.S. I finished this letter and thought you'd be curious about how I looked. I'm around 6-foot-4 and I weigh 195, so I'm not exactly a buff god. I've got brown hair. Brown eyes. I'm into flannel shirts and jeans and T-shirts. I like sitting around in my underwear. I'd love to watch other people sitting around in their underwear... I'm naïve but smart, funny but shy, I've lots of friends but I'm lonely for a buddy that can share my secret.

I have two roommates who would shit if they knew, so you can be "cousin" Frank or something. When you write put Iowa on the return address. I know it seems dumb and paranoid but they're snoops and if it's from Iowa they'll think it's from boring relatives. Anyway tell me every damn thing about you. 'Cuz I'm really curious. Maybe we can go hiking in the hills and go skinny dipping or something corny like that. We're getting a phone on Sunday so I'll give you that later. What do you look like?

Frank, whose real name is Mark Wilhelm, originally placed his personal ad in the *Metro* in November 1989. So it had been out a few months by the time Mark responded, and in that time it had elicited more than 130 written responses. Nevertheless, Mark's was one of the few that really screamed, "Hey, this one really needs to talk," says Wilhelm, who responded to every letter he received, including Mark's, which he responded to on February 14.

"I don't remember very clearly what I wrote," he says. "But I guess that I would have said, 'It sounds as though you're going through some of the same things that I have gone through. I would be happy to talk to you about them. This is a place where you can feel safe and yes, of course I'll keep your secrets.' It was just so obvious that he was so deathly afraid of anybody finding out."

Mark must have been as eager to meet somebody as he suggested in his letter. It was only two days after Mark Wilhelm mailed his response that his phone rang with a call from Mark. And very soon after that Mark rode his bike over to Mark Wilhelm's home. "He was a very handsome young man, with a quick laugh and a smile that would light up a room and make you smile with him," Mark Wilhelm says, adding that Mark, who was "in the kind of condition few of us see past 19," was also quick to shrug off compliments with genuine modesty of the "aw shucks" variety.

Over the next several months, Mark and Mark Wilhelm developed what Wilhelm classifies as a "comforting friendship." The relationship did have a sexual element at times, he says, but neither of them considered it dating. "Most of the time we just sat on the couch and talked or debated things." At the time Mark was working at Anderson's TV near Mark Wilhelm's home and would come over at lunch or at another other time when his roommates, who were Todd Sarner and Cameron Dawson, wouldn't be suspicious.

"I think Mark grew more comfortable being gay when he was over here because he had a chance to hear stories about happy and successful gay people," Mark Wilhelm says. In particular, Wilhelm told Mark about his father's brother, whom he had always known was gay. "I grew up having two uncles who visited me all the time," he says. "And whenever anyone tried to tell me that gay relationships don't work, I knew they didn't know what they were talking about. I'd say, 'My uncles have been together as long as I can remember, so don't try to tell me that.' "

Mark Wilhelm never saw Mark again after Mark returned to Berkeley that fall, but he never forgot the scared 19-year-old who showed up on his doorstep that February afternoon. "The two of us couldn't have been more different in some ways," he says. "I wasn't a sports person by any means, and I was going to [Alcoholics Anonymous], so I was hardly going around pounding beers. But in other ways he was much like I was. I saw so much of myself in him, as far as sexuality goes."

"Mark, it's Tom. I'm just trying to make sure you and Amanda are all right. If you get this message, call at home. I'll be here until about 3. Or try my cell. I'll talk to you later. Bye."

"Hey, what's up, dude? This is Damon. I'm watching this crazy shit on the news. I just wanted to call to make sure you and Amanda were OK. Anyway, give me a call back later. Talk to you later. Bye."

"Mark, hey. It's Seth Davis. It's Tuesday. Don't know if you're in the city. Just checking to see if you're OK, and hopefully you are. Unbelievable tragedy that happened today and just calling the people I know in New York to make sure things are OK. I hope to talk to you soon. Bye."

—the 12th, 13th, and 14th unheard voice-mail messages left on Mark Bingham's mobile phone on Sept. 11, 2001— the first from his friend Tom Street, the second from his friend Damon Billian, and the second from his friend Seth Davis

Clockwise from top: Mark in action on his high school rugby team; Mark as a teenager, and as an adult, in 2001, with his mother, Alice Hoglan.

This page (clockwise): Mark hamming it up for the camera on a trip to Bangkok in 1994; Mark and Paul Holm on an elephant trek in Northern Thailand that same year; Mark and Paul in Ko Pi Pi, Thailand. Opposite page: Mark at a butterfly farm in Thailand; Mark, Paul, and friends Mike Odynski and Mike McGirr relaxing in Provincetown, Mass., 1999.

Top: Mark showing off his playful side in the bathtub.
Bottom: On a trip to Grand Canyon National Park.

*Above: Mark with his first boyfriend, Chris Pratt.
Below: Matt Hall and Mark enjoying Southern
Decadence, a New Orleans gay and lesbian festival.*

Opposite page: Mark at Yosemite National Park on a trip in 1998 for Paul Holm's birthday.
This page: Images from Mark's memorial, held in San Francisco the week after Sept. 11, 2001.
Following page: Mark on a Hong Kong ferry, 1994.

FIVE

MARK RETURNED TO BERKELEY IN THE FALL semester of 1990 with a new understanding of the importance of academics and an appreciation for the amount of time he should spend on his coursework. With a new load of political science–related classes, he started to consider a career in international relations and even talked to friends in the Lodge about taking the foreign-service exam in a couple years. He discovered that the dividends of studying could be measured by more than a higher grade-point average and, in turn, a better job upon graduation.

By hitting the books more often he found he could also assure that he had a better time at parties. The more prepared he was for his classes, he figured, the less he had to worry about them. And the less he had to worry, the easier it was to let loose and have a good time when it came time for a party. This "work hard, play hard" ethic is one Mark had hinted at in his letter to Mark Wilhelm, and it would take an increasingly important role in his life as the years went on. The "Protestant work ethic" his mother had impressed upon him ensured that he would never grow up to be a man who shirked his responsibilities. But now a young man preparing to strike out on his own, Mark knew he never wanted those responsibilities to stand in the way of the more enjoyable things in life.

It was in the pursuit of one of those more enjoyable things in life that, in March 1991, had Mark answering another gay personal ad—this time in the *East Bay Express,* a free weekly from nearby Oakland. "I don't remember the text [of the ad]," says its author, Chris Pratt. "But I'm sure it was something pretty predictable for me like, 'Young furry bruin seeks mate,' or God knows what." A 21-year-old with a dual major in German and English, Chris had been at Cal a year longer than Mark, and like Mark, he had known long before he got to campus that he was gay. Unlike Mark, one of the first things Chris did when he was a freshman was join the undergraduate gay men's support group. "But that didn't go so well," he says, "because everyone was so 'twinkyish.'" Chris was looking for something very specific, and "doing too much speed and dancing at the Pleasuredome until some hunk with hard pecs took me home" was definitely not it.

A burly man with a full beard and a forest of hair on his torso, Chris considered himself a "bear"—a classification whose definition varies depending on whom you're talking to but which most broadly means a gay man who celebrates his masculinity. For example, a bear wouldn't be caught dead with one of the many abdominal-building machines hawked on TV today. If he happens to have a bit of a belly, he wears it proudly. Ads for electrolysis so often targeted at gay men are lost on a bear as well. He would be much more likely to pay for a procedure that added hair to his face, chest, and back—although even that might be too unnatural. And while walking through a standard gay bar can often be an olfactory assault akin to strolling past a fully staffed perfume counter at Bloomingdale's, bars that cater to bears sometimes ban the use of manufactured scents. They prefer a natural musk that is too inherently male to ever be bottled or wrapped with a ribbon.

For Chris, being a bear, in the most general terms, means being "a gay man who is attracted to a beard and perhaps a little extra weight." But at the same time being a bear can mean much more than that, he says, representing an idealized friendship between gay men. "It's not specifically a sexual fetish, in the way some men fetishize Asian women, but it can carry overtones of a deep, warm, loving friendship between men that may be sexual."

If Mark had described his ideal mate, the term "bear" would certainly have been a key element. After all, who better to help him realize the Grizzly Adams fantasy he described in his letter to Mark Wilhelm than Grizzly Adams himself? Amanda Mark remembers that Mark later employed a whole series of words—including but not limited to "course," "thick," "matted," "light," "covering," "tufts," "brushed," "patches of fuzz," "moss-like," and "smooth"—when describing the hair on men's bodies to her. "The words were usually used in combination with each other, as in, 'He had a thick covering of slightly matted back hair,' or 'He had a forest on his stomach,'" Amanda says. "He was especially fond of 'panels,' that bit of hair down the back of the rib cage to the side of the torso."

Mark's attraction to masculinity and body hair, however, was about as close as he came to being considered an actual ursine himself—especially while he was in college. By no means "twinkyish," Mark still hadn't grown into his tall frame. And as far as his facial hair was concerned, he was more than a little frustrated by the fact that he could barely grow a full goatee, let alone a beard. Friends later took to calling Mark "Bear Trap." Despite the physical impediments that blocked him from looking like an actual bear, he found it significantly less difficult to attract those who did.

Mark could tell from Chris's personal ad that he was hoping to meet another bear, and he indicated in his reply that he didn't think he was what Chris was looking for physically. Nevertheless, Chris was excited about the possibility of meeting the rugby-playing frat boy and almost immediately made the first of a series of phone calls between the noticeably skittish Mark and himself. More than a decade later, Chris struggles to remember the specifics of their first dates. "I wish I had kept a journal back then," he says with a sense of frustration. But he couldn't have known at age 21 that the relationship would take on more significance than its simply being his first. Aside from remembering Mark's initial nervousness, Chris says one of the men's first face-to-face meetings was at the campus computer store—Bear Bytes—where he worked at the time. What developed from there was a relationship that lasted about a year and a half. The two of them even lived together for a while—in classic undergraduate style, sharing a studio apartment with Chris's brother and his brother's girlfriend. And when they weren't living together, they sometimes tempted suspicion among Mark's friends by spending the night together in the Lodge, where Mark was now fraternity president and, as one of the perks of the office, had his own bedroom.

"Being with Mark was wonderful because he was such great company, because it was great to meet another gay man who had similar tastes in men, and because he was interested in a lot more than gay life in and of itself," Chris says. "It was fun hanging out at the Lodge with him too. In fact, it was more funny than fun, at first. I wasn't exactly the kind of guy who would ordinarily start to hang out at a fraternity house, and I was afraid that I was going to be surrounded by a bunch of ignorant, drunken, loud guys. But that didn't turn out to be the case at all."

Chris also was fascinated by the idea of meeting "a man who was just at the beginning of sorting out his sexuality." It wasn't that he wanted to mold the way Mark thought about being gay, but because he had been out of the closet for several years—both at school and with his family—Chris was eager to show Mark he could come out without too much pain. The son of a public health worker who made sure he was well-versed in HIV and AIDS issues, Chris also tried to teach Mark everything he thought he should know about safer sex.

Their relationship was about more than how to's, though. There was also a lot of romance, or "mushy stuff," as Mark called it. Particularly mushy was the night Mark turned 21.

Chris took him out for a night on the town, which included flowers and dinner at a Thai restaurant on University Avenue. "It was very Berkeley circa 1991," he remembers. On other days he liked to read to Mark from the copy of Walt Whitman's *Leaves of Grass* he had given him as a gift.

Whitman could be described as the poet laureate of bears, as many of them declare him as their own. And all you have to do is read a little of his work to realize the man was attracted to the same kind of men Mark and Chris liked. "Washes and razors for foofoos," Whitman wrote, "for me, freckles and a bristling beard."

In fact, passages from "Song of Myself," a poem Whitman included in *Leaves of Grass,* were among the young couple's favorites, particularly the two Chris recited from memory when talking about his time with Mark:

Loafe with me on the grass, loose the stop from your
    throat,
Not words, not music or rhyme I want, not customs or
    lecture, not even the best,
Only the lull I like, the hum of your valved voice.
I mind how once we lay, such a transparent summer
    morning,
How you settled your head athwart my hips, and gently
    turn'd over upon me,
And parted the shirt from my bosom-bone, and plunged
    your tongue to my bare-stript hearts,
And reach'd till you felt my beard, and reach'd till you
    held my feet.

And then:

You there, impotent, loose in the knees,
Open your scarf'd chops till I blow grit within you,
Spread your palms and lift the flaps of your pockets,

I am not to be denied, I compel, I have stores plenty and
    to spare
And any thing I have I bestow.

"As dorky as it probably sounds, I really enjoyed reading
Whitman to Mark," Chris says. "And I think it was comforting
to him to read of love for another man in a different context
than, say, *Playguy.*"

Unapologetically less familiar with the great American poets
than Chris, Mark had his own unique way of adding a dash of
mushiness into their relationship. One of his favorites was to
write little notes accompanied by cartoons that looked as if they
were inspired by Matt Groening's "Life in Hell" series—which
was particularly popular at the time. The cartoons, which Chris
says Mark "drew all the time," demonstrated that, like Chris, he
was clearly excited this new relationship. In a note he faxed
Chris on Aug. 13, 1992, for example, he drew a cartoon bear
wearing a SEVERED HEADS SUCK T-shirt, making fun of one of
Chris's favorite bands, an Australian electronic group called
Severed Heads. Then next to the bear he wrote, "Dear
Christopher: Todd will pick me up at 5:00 P.M. I'll call you
tonite. I love you and I don't know why. Thanks for driving me
to work. I wish that you would have molested me this morning
(sigh). Yer pal, Mark."

Other of Mark's cartoons reflected the confusion, concern,
and exhilaration Mark must have felt taking these first steps as
a gay man. In one of them he drew two couples, which again
happened to be bears, under the heading "Homosexual vs.
Heterosexual, Pros and Cons." The pros and cons he listed next
to the gay bears included: share clothing; know what the other
likes; AIDS; commitment; New Age people find you fascinat-
ing; one doesn't have to support the other; guilt; no good tax
write-off; don't need separate deodorant; and have trouble
fumbling with prophylactics. Next to the straight bears he
wrote: social acceptance; can make babies; don't have to tell

mom; AIDS; commitment; guilt; often have to treat partner with kid gloves 'cos you don't know how they work; have natural lubricant; and have trouble with prophylactics. Most of all, though, the cartoons, which became a staple of most of Mark's written correspondence with his friends, were a reflection of his sense of humor.

A year and half into the relationship, however, Chris decided to call it quits. Mark was simply not bearish enough for him. "As much as I loved him, I had always had a fantasy in the back of my mind that I would one day meet a bear myself," Chris says. "At the end of it, I decided that I really should try to strike out on my own in search of a particular kind of sexual experience that I wasn't getting with Mark. You know, the big, hairy, bearded man kind of thing."

Their breakup wasn't one of those in which one partner says to the other, "I'll never see you again. Our love is no more," Chris says. In fact the two of them even lived together again as roommates later on. But Chris knew Mark was hurt by his decision to end it. "It's never easy when you fall in love with someone and they let you know that it's not quite right for them," he acknowledges. And for Mark, the pain was likely compounded by the fact that this breakup wasn't exactly the kind of thing he could bring up over drinks with his buddies at the Lodge.

At least he didn't think he could. Mark—who was still scared to death about how his friends would react if they figured out his secret—didn't know that many of his fraternity brothers had already started to ask themselves, and each other, if he might be gay. The question first came up at the Lodge when word spread that someone had spotted Mark at one of the gay bars in San Francisco's South of Market district. SoMa bars had a reputation for attracting a less fey and otherwise more alternative gay crowd than the more popular Castro district, and Mark sometimes stopped by some of them, including the Stud, which according to Todd Sarner was popular among closeted Cal students at the time; Rawhide II, a country-western dance club; and the Lone Star, one of the city's better-known bear hangouts.

For many closeted gay men and lesbians, entering a gay bar for the first time can be exponentially more frightening than giving a speech in front of an auditorium full of strangers. However, just as it's said that people who fear public speaking can calm their nerves before a speech by imagining audience members in their underwear, closeted gay men and women can ease their fear of being discovered in a gay bar by telling themselves that anyone who sees them there must have the same secret they do. So in other words, why worry? But that didn't work for Mark. What happened instead, as Dave Kupiecki explains, is that a bouncer at one of the bars happened to not only be a former Cal football player but also a very indiscreet friend of several Chi Psi members who played for the team.

But the rumors spread by the bouncer weren't the only thing that set off Dave's gaydar with regard to Mark. "This was one of my best friends in the fraternity, and I knew his circle of friends," he explains. "And then all the sudden he moves out and starts living with a guy named Chris, who none of us has ever heard of. I think most of the guys just kind of blew it off and didn't think much about it at the time. But it didn't click with me. I was like, *Wait a second here. What's going on?*" Chris's omnipresence also helped raise some questions for Amanda. "Mark wrote me a big letter that was full of 'Chris, blah, blah, blah,' and 'Chris, Chris, Chris,' and I had to ask myself, *Is Chris a boy or a girl?* And when I finally figured out Chris was a guy, I thought, *Ooooh!*"

The choreography of his coming out had to be planned very carefully, and it's clear Mark analyzed every detail of it. At a small Chi Psi party in 1991, Stephanie Stark was surprised to see him wearing a T-shirt with crude homophobic references on it. She didn't know Mark was gay, but she did know he wasn't bigoted—and she told him so. "I just laid into him," she says. "I told him I thought he was a better person than that and that I was disappointed in him. And he just looked at me like I was crazy." About an hour later, Mark asked Stephanie to go outside with him. "I have to tell you something," he said when they left the house. "I'm gay, and I wore this shirt to see what kind of reaction I'd get. I wanted to see who thought it was funny and who thought it was offensive." He then told Stephanie that she was the first of his friends and family members who he had come out to. "He was just so afraid," Stephanie says. "He told me, 'I have so much to think about and I have so much to deal with.' And I realized that night what an amazingly strong person he was and how brilliant it was to be testing the waters with that shirt."

Buoyed by Stephanie's response, Mark came out to Todd Sarner in the spring of 1991 as they sat in a car across the street from the Good Guys electronics store in Emeryville, Calif., where they both worked at the time. "Mark was sitting in the passenger seat acting very nervous, and he didn't get nervous about many things," Todd says. "Then he just blurted, 'I need to tell you something...I'm gay.'" Surprised by the news, Todd could only think to ask, "When did this happen?"

Mark, who kidded Todd about that question for the next 10 years, explained that he had known most of his life that he was gay. Then he turned the tables with a question that was posed as a joke but could have easily been prompted by innocent optimism, asking Todd, "Are you gay too?" Todd came out as straight and then, as he looked over to the passenger seat, recognized the same lug he had known growing up. Mark's nervousness was gone "and I could see immediately the huge relief he felt about being able to come out." Todd felt good too. "It was an incredible day," he says.

That night, as the longtime friends racked up an $80 beer tab (which is more than 12 beers apiece at 1991 prices) at a local bar, Todd tried to make sense of what Mark had told him. How could he know someone so well for so long and not know so much about him? "I thought, *Didn't Mark have sex with that girl?*

And then I remembered that he didn't. *And what about that other girl?* No," he says. "At that moment it was as if all the planets were aligning and the clouds were parting. Finally it all became clear to me why this attractive, intelligent, sociable guy never really dated."

One person he had yet to test the waters with was his mother. Even though Alice worked with many gay men in her job as a flight attendant, she says she was "vaguely antigay" at that time. Any "anti" thoughts she had, however, were based much less in disapproval of gay and lesbian people than they were in the fact that she simply didn't think about them very much. Mark always tried to protect his mother by not telling her details about his life that he thought might upset her. These details ranged everywhere from the incident at the airport in New Zealand when he crashed through the plate-glass window to the fact that he smoked cigarettes. But by August 1991, his relationship with Chris and his comfort with being gay had progressed to a point where he no longer wanted to keep such a huge chunk of himself—his sexual orientation—a secret from his mother.

It had only been a year and a half since he had said that his family members would never learn about his sexual orientation because, as he wrote to Mark Wilhelm, "No matter how much explaining I did it couldn't be the same relationship that I have now." His life had changed immeasurably in the 19 months since he wrote that letter, but the fear of damaging his 21-year relationship with his mother was still very real. There was a knot in his stomach whenever he thought about it. Even if she reacted to the news by saying all the right things—such as, "You're still my son" and "I love you no matter what"—wouldn't it still alter the way she looked at him? He wondered how, in her eyes, a gay son could be the same son she had watched grow up.

The best approach, he decided, was to spend a day so packed

with quality mother-son time that when he finally popped the announcement there would be no question that he was still the same Mark. So that late-summer day he and his mother tooled around California's Sonoma County in Alice's station wagon. As far as Alice remembers, there wasn't anything remarkable about the day. "I was grousing to him about some fella I was dating at the time, and we were having a pretty run-of-the-mill conversation," she says. "I was just loving being with my son that day and regretting that we didn't get to see so much of each other anymore." Then, as the end of evening approached and the sun, in its last gasp of the day, blasted blindingly through their windshield, Mark very tentatively said, "Mom, I have something to tell you, and I've promised myself that I was going to tell you before the sun went down."

Alice immediately knew her son had something serious to tell her, and she could tell that, as he continued to talk about things she can't begin to remember today, he was trying to soften the blow. Then, just as quickly as the sky can change its colors once the sun finally sets, Mark said, "I'm gay."

"I was flabbergasted and really thrown for a loop," Alice recalls. "I really don't have much in common with what I guess you would call the militant fringe, and I had entertained stereotypes about gay people. Now I was faced with the fact that my son was gay and that he was telling me so. It certainly was not news that I welcomed." After guiding her through the initial shock, Mark left Alice alone for a few weeks to process the information. "He didn't pin me down or ask me how I felt," she says. "And that gave me a chance to figure out how to respond."

Chris's parents, who were among the first people Alice talked to after Mark came out, helped her sort through the news simply by talking with her about sexual orientation and the role it played in people's lives. "I realized that I didn't go around saying, 'I'm Alice Hoglan, I'm a heterosexual,' and that Mark's identity didn't really change who he was," she says. Alice also went to see a counselor, who told her that the confusion and sense of mourning she was feeling was normal. "My counselor told me that no mother ever wants to hear that her son is gay," she says. "But then I realized that there is no one I would have rather heard the words 'and I'm gay' from than my son."

With his mother, Stephanie, and Todd behind him, Mark began the sporadic process of coming out to each of his friends. Amanda heard the news through the grapevine. More surprised that Mark hadn't told her yet than she was to confirm her suspicions about his sexual orientation, she tried to set the stage for Mark to come out to her. The night in May 1992 when she and Mark met at Bonnie Dune beach seemed to be just right. As they sat with their toes in the cold sand, only getting up every once in a while to throw a stick on the bonfire, Amanda made every attempt to stoke their conversation with references to her gay friends in Sydney and all the fun she had been having with them.

Mark didn't bite, but he got the message. And the next night when he and Amanda where hanging out in Berkeley, he finally asked, "You know I'm gay, right?" Posed the way it was, his question suggested that Mark assumed Amanda would have heard by now, but he was actually shocked when Amanda acknowledged that she did know. "How did you find out?" he asked. Choosing not to rat on her friends, Amanda instead listed all the reasons she had assumed he was gay. "Finally I just said, 'It's just obvious!'" And Mark, as she remembers, let out a huge sigh of relief.

As obvious as it was to Amanda that Mark was gay, she didn't realize how frightened he still was about other people finding out. Then that summer, as she worked as a camp counselor in Santa Cruz, Amanda started to join Mark on trips to San Francisco and to the SoMa and Castro gay bars. "If we ran into anyone—even if it was somebody he only thought he might know—he grabbed my hand and pretended that I was his girlfriend," she says. "I always asked him, 'What do you think they're doing here?' and 'Don't you think they're probably gay too?' But I really didn't mind. I could tell he was still having a hard time, and if my being there with him made it any easier for him, that was fine with me."

Coming out was heavy on Mark's mind, but it hardly consumed him. Chris Pratt remembers that even when they first started dating, Mark's priorities never really strayed from rugby and his fraternity friends. And even though Amanda was one of the few people in whom he had confided, Mark's sexuality was hardly the focus of all their conversations. He and Amanda were much more likely to challenge each other to a match of Super Mario Brothers or drive across the South in a 1976 Cadillac Sedan deVille, as they did over Christmas break in 1992.

"A couple friends of mine from Australia and I bought the car for $670 and drove it from San Francisco down to Mexico and across to New Orleans, where Mark met us," Amanda says. After New Orleans, Mark and the girls realized they didn't have enough money for hotels, so they stayed in Chi Psi fraternity houses in Atlanta and Chapel Hill, N.C. Then, when they got to Washington, D.C., where his fraternity has no chapter, Mark came up with another plan: "We went to a [Sigma Alpha Epsilon] house, and he said, 'Hi, I'm Mark Bingham. My brother is an SAE. Can we stay here?'" The ruse worked, but Mark, Amanda, and her friends got what they paid for. "Their house was even more heinous than the Lodge," Amanda remembers. "They had hosted a New Year's Eve party a few nights earlier and still hadn't cleaned up." As far as Amanda knows, a souvenir picked up from this trip is still hanging up at the Lodge in Berkeley: a framed composite photograph from the Chi Psi house in Chapel Hill, where each of the members wore velvet and pearls rather than the more traditional suits and ties.

As hilarious as he found the gender-bending fraternity photo, as he brought it back to the Lodge after Christmas break Mark couldn't help wonder again how open-minded his brothers were. How would they take it if he came out to them? Since he had made plans to share a house with Todd and Dave Kupiecki that semester, Dave became the first Chi Psi Mark came out to. By this time, however, Dave says he too had already figured out the name of his friend's game. When Mark finally told Dave, he reacted with the same nonchalance Amanda had. And, again like Amanda, he explained to Mark how he knew. He also told Mark that the topic of his sexual orientation had become a bit of a behind-the-scenes debate in the Lodge. "Certain guys were still saying, 'No way.' But by that point, many of us thought it was pretty likely," he says.

After his conversation with Dave, Mark decided it was time to make one giant announcement. So he planned a party at the Berkeley home he, Todd, and Dave shared, and invited all of his friends. Everyone assumed this was just going to be another one of the blowouts Mark was famous for—kegs, beer bongs, and a good time all around. But halfway into what turned out to be an all-night party that stretched into the not so early morning, Mark gathered all his friends in one room and made the announcement. He also tried to make it clear that he was the same guy they had always known. They just knew more about him now.

"Mark was pretty adamant about never being labeled as anything," Todd explains. "He was proud of who he was, but he wanted everyone to know he was still the same Mark. And people had always looked up to him so much that when he came out that night, I watched some gears turn in the heads of some pretty homophobic people. You could see them trying to reconcile the Mark they knew with what he had just told them. You could see these people say to themselves, *Wait a minute. Mark's gay, and he doesn't fit any of my stereotypes of what a gay man is. So maybe it's my stereotypes that are wrong.*"

Actually, for many of the people who were there that night, Mark's announcement confirmed what they had already assumed. "Those of us who hadn't already been told kind of suspected it because he had never really dated a girl and because now and then he'd come back to the fraternity with a guy and go to his room and lock the door," says Chi Psi member and friend Spencer Kelly. "I think he expected it to have this huge impact, like he expected a lot of people to react to it negatively. But, with a few exceptions, none of us did."

One of those exceptions was a young fraternity brother who had idolized Mark and had become something of a little brother to him. As Dave remembers it, the young man arrived at about 6 A.M., well after Mark's announcement but not too late to hear about it in one of the half-dozen huddled conversations the party had dissolved to by then. "When he heard that Mark was gay, he just turned and left," Dave says. "And I don't think he talked to Mark for months."

At the time, Mark thought Spencer was one of the exceptions that night as well. "He told me that years later. He thought I was more narrow-minded than I am," Spencer says. "I had a number of gay friends before then, and I still have a number of close gay friends—partly because of Mark. And I have come to find that many of them are better friends than straight people. In fact, most of them are better friends because they make better companions."

However, the most legendary reaction Mark got after coming out that night was from his fraternity brother Don Cotter. The 6-foot-7, 350-pound Cal football player, whose mix-pitched voice sounded a lot like the character Barney from *The Simpsons,* said, "So, dude, do you like me?" When Mark explained that he wasn't attracted to Don, Don persisted. "Come on, dude, come on. Don't you find me attractive?" When Mark finally relented, lied to Don, and told him that he did find him attractive, Don answered, "Cool, but don't touch me!"

It felt as if the weight of the closet was now almost completely off his back, but that didn't mean life changed a whole lot for Mark. He didn't want it to. As his friends realized the night of the party, Mark was happy being a rugby player, he was happy being a fraternity brother, he was happy being a student, he was happy being a son, and he was happy being a gay man. Coming out wasn't his effort to change any of that. Instead, it was his attempt to assure that some day he could fully integrate these different sides of his life with one another. He had figured out that his fear of being discovered in a gay bar was as irrational as if he had been afraid of being discovered on the rugby field. Fresh out of the closet, he was definitely eager to meet new friends and enjoy new experiences, but none of them would come at the expense of those in his life that were already tried and true.

"Hey, Mark. This is Owen Robertson. I'm just calling because one of the flights that was down today was from New York to San Francisco. And I know you left yesterday, but I was just calling just to see if you're OK.... Hope you're doing well. Bye."

"Mark, hey. It's Derrick. We of course have heard the news about what's going on in New York, and we wanted to make sure you're OK. So if you could just give us a quick call back...we would appreciate it. A couple guys are asking about it. I hope you're OK and God bless. Bye."

"Hey, Mark. It's Bryce. Just calling to check up on you and also to let you know that a couple guys on the rugby team have kind of put out feelers on the Web site and just wanted to know how you are. So, if you could just shoot a message to the Fog or let me know you're OK and I'll forward the message. That would be great. Talk to you soon. Bye-bye."

—the 15th, 16th, and 17th unheard voice-mail messages left on Mark Bingham's mobile phone on Sept. 11, 2001— the first from his friend Owen Robertson, the second from his San Francisco Fog rugby teammate Derrick Mickle, and the third from his Fog teammate Bryce Eberhart

As much as Mark's friends say he eschewed labels, the 23-year-old found himself struggling to find an identity when he graduated from the University of California in the spring of 1993. The differences between being a student at Cal and being an alum of the university were much more vast than going to classes one day and then not doing so the next. Suddenly Mark was being measured by a different standard, where his success required more than acing a test, pulling off the best luau party in history, or even winning a national championship in rugby. Armed with a bachelor's degree in social sciences, with an emphasis in international relations, Mark had to ask himself, *What now?*

The answers to that question had come much easier when he had imagined himself as a college graduate two years before. Personally, things were going well with Chris Pratt and seemed as though they would continue to. And professionally, Mark planned to take the foreign-service exam and hopefully land a job in international relations. When it came time to graduate, though, he and Chris were only friends, and Mark had failed the foreign-service exam.

Socially, he was still a star among his friends. Coming out as a gay man to so many of them in his last year at Cal hadn't done a thing to change his standing as the center of most their attention. He was still a sucker for a game of pickup basketball with the boys, could be counted on for the best color commentary during televised sporting events—especially if his favorite teams, the Miami Dolphins or the Atlanta Braves, were playing—and although he had yet to discover the virtues of what was to become his favorite alcoholic drink, the cosmopolitan, by most accounts he still could drink most of his friends under the table.

Now that he no longer worried as much about who saw him at gay clubs, he was, for the first time, comfortably sending new friends under tables in Castro and SoMa bars. Notable among his new acquaintances were a couple he had met one night at the country-western dance club Rawhide II, Steven Gold and Bill Hollywood. Steven, an allergist, and Bill, a retail manager who'd grown up in Texas, had been together four years. Because they were happily coupled, they didn't go out on the town too often. Most of the San Francisco gay nightlife scene, they found, was solidly structured around the pursuit of other men, which was something they weren't interested in. Rawhide was different, however, because the dance floor provided an activity they could enjoy as a couple. And, of course, the country music appealed to the Texan in Bill.

On a July night, Steven and Bill were stationed at a bar behind the dance floor drinking snake-bite shots when Mark strode over and very directly introduced himself to Bill, who just happened to be the one of the two with a beard. "He started hitting on Bill a little bit," Steven says. "And then Bill, as either of us always did when someone hit on us, turned to me and said, 'This is my lover, Steven.'

"Unlike most men in a similar situation, who either stopped talking or tried to somehow come between us when they learned we were a couple, Mark immediately directed his attention to both of us. Of course, he had good taste in men and was attracted to Bill. But when he learned we were a committed couple, he wanted to be our friend. He wanted to know about our lives. So a couple of shots later we invited him over for hamburgers and hot dogs the next day, which was the Fourth of July. He was just too charming to resist."

The "cowbears," as Mark started to call Bill and Steven, became both friends and role models for Mark from that point on. And it wasn't long before he introduced them to the key people in his life. "I remember going to the Rawhide with Bill and Steven one drunken night," Todd Sarner says. "Amanda was there too, and we were all drinking tequila. Then I started line dancing with Mark and ended up slow dancing with Bill." It was bizarre, Todd remembers, but not because he was being led around a dance floor by a tall, bearded gay man, but because the two of them were dancing to country music. "I never really got into country," he says.

Mark became an equally important friend to Steven and Bill. He crashed at their house when he needed a place to stay, and he ate whatever they had in their refrigerator when he was hungry—which was most of the time, as they remember. "One time he came over after we had been away for a week, pulled this sweet potato pie of Bill's out of the refrigerator, and said, 'Dude, this is great. I especially like the green stuff.'" When Steven realized Mark was talking about a mold that was blanketing the dish, he grabbed the pie from his hands and threw it in the trash. "You would have thought he was a child and I had just taken away his favorite toy. He didn't mind that he was eating mold. He only cared that it was good-tasting mold."

Mark came to forge such a strong bond with Steven and Bill that he started to refer to them as his "gay parents" and his "fairy godfathers." Even though Mark had come out to Alice, there are some things no son wants to discuss with his mother. And this was especially the case with Mark, who still had a strong desire to protect his mother, whether that meant not discussing his difficulties in dating or deciding against calling her when he hurt himself in rugby. He could comfortably do all of that with Steven and Bill. And they in turn tried to be father figures for Mark. They even took him to buy his first-ever suit when he graduated from Cal. Bill still laughs when recounting how much Mark squirmed when his measurements were being taken. "They didn't have anything that fit him at any of the department stores," he says. "But we did eventually find something at the big and tall store."

Bill and Steven represented more than parental figures for Mark, though. The commitment, compassion, and longevity of their relationship was everything he wanted to have himself. "He wanted the kind of relationship that Bill and I have," Steven says. "He wanted a strong man. Of course, the guy's physical attributes were important to him. But in the end, he wanted a strong man. And we wanted that for him too." In October 1993, Mark showed Steven and Bill just how much he respected their relationship with a poem he painted on canvas and presented them with for their sixth anniversary:

Strength, a fortress, two men
With a love each day that waxes stronger
With paths that crossed
When all seem lost
Paths now joined that stretch e'en longer.

Love exists outside of science
Where rules of thumb do not apply
Measure, squint at love's defiance
Physics, math; to love a tie.

So some can question, wonder, doubt
Reject the truth of synergy
The rules of thumb
Now deaf and dumb
'Cause one and one can still make three.

What joyous thing to be a man
That loves a man with body same
To name it love, pure white, a dove
While some can spite or wield shame.

This happy mix of words details
A bridge that spans a gorge so wide
But none can sway, nor even shake
This finest love, that manly pride.

Two months later, at Steven and Bill's annual Christmas party, Mark took a chance on a little romance himself. He first noticed Paul Holm, a tall, bearded 32-year-old, as they were standing on opposite sides of a table topped with Bill's famous brisket and other assorted holiday dishes. Paul noticed Mark as well: He remembers watching him inhale a serving bowl full of appetizers before striding over, sticking out his hand and with a big grin, saying, "Hi, I'm Mark Bingham. Who are you?" The two of them spent the rest of the evening talking about a number of things, not the least of which were their equal passions for University of California athletics; Paul also had gone to school at Berkeley. "My first impression was that here was a guy who was very charismatic, outgoing, and gregarious. And I think his size contributed to that impression," Paul says. "At the same time, I could also tell that he was very aware of whether the people around him were comfortable and having a good time. He wanted people to like him, whether it was someone he had just met or someone he had known for a long time."

At 7 o'clock the next morning Mark's voice on the answering machine woke Paul up. "I don't know if you remember me," the voice said. "It's Mark from last night, and I wanted to see if you wanted to get together today." He couldn't meet Mark that day, but they did get together a couple days later. And, as Paul remembers, they started seeing each other immediately. Within months, Mark had all but moved into Paul's San

Francisco home at 14th and Noe Street. The ensuing relation-ship was "very intense and wonderful," Paul says. "We did everything from sitting in front of the TV watching football, which we did all the time, to other stay-at-home stuff like play-ing Scrabble or cards." Cal games were also a big part of their lives, since Paul had season tickets to the home football and basketball games.

"Mark was pretty conservative at that point, especially in terms of how he approached guys," Paul says, "so I don't think what we shared was very typical for him." Actually, it wasn't typical for Mark in a lot of ways. Nine years his senior, Paul had a law degree, was well established as a businessman, and could afford to live a life of fine dining, wine, and travel. Mark, on the other hand, had not too long ago been living in a garage in Berkeley, where he had to stretch an extension cord from the main house in order to have electricity. And, as Paul points out, Mark's idea of good meal when they first met "was to put all the leftovers in a blender and make a leftover shake." Now he lived in a well-appointed home just blocks away from San Francisco's Castro district and had graduated from blending up leftovers to distinguishing between an aged Bordeaux and a California cabernet.

The changes appealed to Mark on a number of levels. First, through Paul he could prove to himself, his friends, and his family that two men could have a committed relationship. And second, on a possibly less conscious level, his relationship with Paul helped fill the identity void left just months prior by his graduation from Cal. Now when he asked himself, *What now?* he knew that he was living that "what now" in a very grown-up relationship with Paul.

Mark was much less enthusiastic about the progress of his professional life. Since graduating he had worked as a customer service representative for a cell phone company. And while he had yet to settle on what exactly he wanted to do with himself career-wise, his experience in this job more than confirmed that customer service wasn't it. After sitting through several informational interviews with some of Paul's friends, and after recognizing that he obviously had strong people skills, Mark started to consider public relations as a career. And soon after he started to examine the field he learned about an internship opportunity with the hi-tech PR company Alexander Communications.

Holland Carney has a vivid memory of the day in 1994 when she interviewed Mark for the internship. "The gig was that the interns would work for three months at $10 an hour. If everything worked out, there was a 99% chance that we would offer them a job," she says. "But Mark was a tough negotiator, and he expressed in very plain terms that taking an hourly job was a step back for him. I, however, really wanted him. And I remember thinking, *There's a lot of potential here. Obviously this guy's really assertive.* So I got tough myself, said 'That's the deal,' and somehow talked him into accepting the job."

Three months later, Mark was offered a job as assistant account manager. Six months after that he was promoted to account manager. And another six months after that he became a senior account manager. "We are talking about a period of time when we were working on the first-ever commercialization of the Internet, and there was nobody out there who had 20 years' experience doing this work," Holland says. "We needed people who were smart and who could think strategically, and Mark had that. In fact, the core of his strength—and I think this was true throughout his life—was that he knew how to respond when faced with the unexpected."

His responsibilities included promoting products for some of Alexander's clients, including Novel and Hewlett-Packard. For HP, he was charged with getting the media to notice OmniGo, one of the earliest versions of the handheld computer. "We took the account over from another agency that had done a crappy job on its launch. And now we had to get press for a product that had already been on the market for three or four months,"

Holland says. "I asked Mark, 'Do you really think we can do it?' And I can still see his face. He just got so excited. And he did it. OmniGo had a real nifty design, so he made that his hook. Then he got some great photographs of it taken, made friends with every reporter who did reviews of handheld computers, and got them to write about it. He worked his butt off."

Mark loved the work, and when he got a media "hit" for one of his products—especially if that hit was, for example, above the fold in *The Wall Street Journal*'s Marketplace section—he would literally jump up and down at his desk. "We used to call him Tigger because he got so excited," Holland says. "If I think of all the people I've known in my life and all the people I've worked with, I'd say he's one of the top five in terms of being able to say every day, 'I love what I do.' I think that's a pretty significant thing to be able to say about a person."

Mark's passion for his work was reflected in Alexander's appreciation of him and the resulting 25%–30% salary hikes he earned almost every six months. "These were the boom years," Holland says. "And for the effective people who really stuck with their jobs, there was some real money to be made."

The salary helped establish Mark as more of an equal financial partner in his relationship with Paul, and together they took his "work hard, play hard" ethic to a new level. He and Paul became regulars at some of the city's finest restaurants. They even started to record their different dining experiences in wine journals—remarking on everything from the quality of the food and the wine to the ambience and the quality of service. They began to travel extensively as well. Mark had taken his first trip to Europe with Todd Sarner in 1990, when the two of them went to a Pink Floyd concert in commemoration of the collapse of the Berlin Wall. He went again with Chris Pratt the following year. But money was enough of a concern on those trips that Mark didn't experience the continent's finer offerings until he and Paul made the first of their annual pilgrimages to France in 1994.

Usually spending a week in Paris and an additional week in Normandy, Brittany, the Loire Valley, Bordeaux, Provence, or Dordogne, the two of them explored the museums, roamed the vineyards, and sometimes just wandered the streets. France for Mark and Paul became one of the few places they could relax, tickle their culinary fancies, and revel in each other's company far away from the hassles of home.

"We particularly liked Paris in the fall," Paul says. "We just walked for hours exploring the city." Sometimes they walked too far. One day they went on a tour of the city's sewer system without realizing they were about to explore the city's actual working sewer. "We were horrified," Paul says. "By the end I had to run out, and I actually got sick. Mark loved telling people about that."

They also made frequent trips to New York City, where Paul was often called for work and Mark would meet him for extended weekends. It was in New York that the couple had one of their most romantic evenings, while dining downtown at the classic French-style restaurant Chanterelle. It started off as just one of their better gastronomic experiences, when the restaurant's owner took a liking to them and filled their table with his best appetizers. Then Mother Nature turned the intensity up a notch or two by throwing in late-summer lightning. "The restaurant was almost all glass, and we were the last ones there by then," Paul says. "The staff turned off the lights, and Mark and I just sat in the dining room alone watching this amazing 20-minute lightning storm. That night kind of crystallized a lot of New York for us."

On nights like that, Mark and Paul spent as much time chewing the fat of each other's lives as they did relishing the food and wine. One frequent topic of discussion was how much of their personal lives they should share with clients and colleagues. "The consensus between us with regard to clients was that it was rarely a plus, and that it could sometimes be a negative, to be openly gay," Paul says. "That was just the hard economic reality of it." They were similarly private about their relationship when they met people out socially. "We went to all kinds of events together," Paul explains. "But we didn't send out proclamations about our sexual orientation. We just let people think or say what they would."

Friends remember that Mark, who put so much emphasis during his last years of college on coming out to his friends and loved ones, was somewhat troubled by this new economic reality. But according to Paul, Mark acknowledged that it was just part of life. "For him it was about being as sensitive on the business front as he was with his family members." After he came out to Alice, for example, Mark only told other family members that he was gay when he thought they were ready for the information. Even though Alice knew and loved Paul and understood the nature of his relationship with her son, as far as other family members were concerned Paul was, first, Mark's friend and, later, roommate, before it was acknowledged that they were life partners. Mark handled things the same way at work, Paul says, only telling clients and coworkers about his personal life when he thought it was necessary or when he was certain it wouldn't hurt the nature of their professional relationship.

One of the few people Mark was open with at Alexander about being gay was another gay man himself, Ken Montgomery. The two of them were students at Cal together but never met until well after graduation, one Sunday night at a San Francisco bar called the Eagle. Mark recognized Ken from his stint as the "mike man," the guy who leads cheers at the Cal football games. So he naturally went up and introduced himself. Within minutes of the introduction, Ken realized that he recognized Mark too, from his less official exploits on the Cal football field. In addition to Mark's run-in with the University of Wisconsin mascot, Ken particularly remembered an incident at the 1992 standoff between Cal and cross-bay rival Stanford University, when Mark ran onto the field and tackled Stanford's flag bearer. "That guy with the flag was massive," Ken says. "And even though I didn't know Mark at the time, I clearly remember watching him and saying to myself, *Man, that guy's got a death wish!*" The Berkeley police were equally taken by Mark's performance and arrested him, just as they had when he tried to tackle the University of Wisconsin mascot three years earlier.

After their meeting at the Eagle, Mark turned Ken on to Alexander and the two became colleagues. "We had such a competitive relationship there. We wanted to see who got promoted first, who got raises first, and who got the biggest raises," says Ken, who worked with Mark on a number of accounts, including Novell. "But it wasn't an unhealthy, negative thing. It was like brothers would do. We were just a couple of young guys who were sprouting our professional horns at the same time."

Both big guys with similar senses of humor, Mark and Ken fed off each other at work. Either of them could send the other into hysterics—often by reciting lines from an old movie they'd seen together. "I'm not kidding you. We would walk out of a hugely important meeting and just start quoting from *Carrie*," Ken says. "I'd say, 'Mark, I can see your dirty pillows.' And without missing a beat, he'd turn to me and say, 'They're breasts, Mama, and every girl has them!'"

Their bond was strengthened by business trips to Chicago or Atlanta, where Mark and Ken sometimes wiggled their way out of many group functions so they could hit Halsted Street or Midtown. And like he did with Paul, Mark talked with Ken about being openly gay at work. "He was just concerned that people would treat him differently if they knew, and that it would block advancement," Ken says. "I told him what every single gay person says after they come out: 'Staying in the closet is really a big waste. It's just a lot of pressure you really don't need.'"

Just as Mark's fraternity brothers had figured out the truth behind Chris Pratt's visits to the Lodge, many of

Mark's colleagues correctly deciphered the nature of his relationship with Paul. And Holland Carney, who is a lesbian, says she was initially troubled by the fact that Mark didn't talk to her about his being gay. "I never went around the office and said, 'Hi, I'm a big lesbian!' But I did have a picture of my partner on my desk—because I was in a leadership position and I thought it was important that people realized diversity was an important part of our organization," she says. "After someone told me that Mark was gay, I remember having a conversation with a coworker and asking, 'I wonder if I'm doing something wrong as a manager if, as out as I am, Mark doesn't feel like he can be.'" Like Paul, however, Carney drew a distinction when it came to clients. "While I was extremely out at work, I was only selectively out with clients," she says. Nevertheless, she adds, the Silicon Valley and San Francisco public relations world was a much more understanding environment than many people realize. "It was very much a meritocracy that was truly about what you can do and what you can contribute and not a lot about that other bullshit."

Holland probably would have had more confidence in her management skills if she had known that it wasn't only when he was at work that Mark fumbled over the appropriate approach to disclosing his sexual orientation to new people in his life. Mike McGirr met Mark after the two of them shared a flight from Salt Lake City to Oakland and then wound up on the same Bay Area Rapid Transit car into San Francisco. "There was this family on the train that was going into the city during their layover, and I heard them asking Mark for a few suggestions of places they might see." Upon hearing Mark recommend Fisherman's Wharf, Mike, who had only lived in San Francisco for a few months, interrupted to suggest a few "less touristy" sites. "When we got off the train Mark asked if I wanted to get a beer," Mike says. "And then he said, 'Dude, when tourists ask you for something to do, send them to a tourist zone. Don't send them to the nice neighborhoods. It ruins it for the rest of us.'"

Over the next several weeks, Mike and Mark met for beers after work a half-dozen times. And before each visit, Mark asked Mike where he wanted to meet. "I'd say, 'I don't know. I'm not from here.' We always ended up going to some nondescript bar," Mike says. One night Mark said he wanted to introduce Mike to some friends. And when they met at another generic downtown tavern, Mike asked where Mark's friends were. "Oh, they're at another bar, where I want to take you," Mark replied. Then, as he fumbled for words, he said, "I don't mean to offend you, but are you gay?" Mike, who thought the unspoken was nonetheless assumed, answered yes, and then Mark said, "Oh, OK. I'm gay too."

A few weeks later Mark introduced Mike to Paul, and the three of them immediately hit it off and, as Mike remembers, started to spend almost every weekend night together. "They were my best friends in the city," he says. One particular night they hit almost every bar in the Castro and were heading down a side street to yet another—"I think it was the Jackhammer," Mike says—when two men jumped out from behind a van and demanded, "Give us your money!" When one of the would-be muggers brandished a gun, Mike immediately threw his wallet on the ground. But an infuriated Mark lunged at the guy, wrestled him to the ground, and wrenched his wrist until the gun flew out of his hand and into the street. Meanwhile, the guy without the gun ran, knocking both Paul and Mike off their feet as he dashed out of sight. "Then we looked up, and Mark was still pummeling [the first guy]. He was just beating him to a pulp," Mike says. After Mike and Paul convinced Mark to let up, the first would-be mugger ran away as well.

The trio spent the next several hours in a San Francisco police car, unsuccessfully searching for their attackers. And as they zigzagged through the city, both Mike and Paul told Mark several times that he should have been more careful—especially since the guy was carrying a gun. But that didn't make sense to Mark. "I had to protect you guys," he said. "I had to protect my friends."

It wasn't unusual for Mark, who was still playing club-level rugby in the city, to come into the office the day after a particularly rough match with cuts and scrapes. But his coworkers were particularly concerned when he came in the morning after the mugging. When Holland and her boss, Pam Alexander, learned that his two black eyes were the result of several blows to the head from the butt of a gun, they too warned him to be more careful. "Here we were, these two older women, saying, 'Mark, you've got to be a little less bold in these kinds of situations. You could really get hurt,'" Holland says. "But his attitude was, 'What the fuck? If these guys jump me, I'm not just going to take it.'"

Holland found Mark to be equally headstrong when he thought he wasn't getting a fair shake at work, as was the case in 1997, after he had been with the firm for a couple years. By this time Alexander had doubled in size, from 15 employees to more than 35, and Holland had hired a vice president who helped supervise a number of those employees, including Mark. "He didn't like that especially well," she remembers. "He felt that he should still be under my direct report." When his new supervisor decided against extending a raise that Mark thought he was due, Mark barked, "I don't give a shit what you say" and took his case to Holland.

"He wasn't as mad as he was frustrated," Holland says. "You know how in every picture of him you see today he's got that huge smile on his face? Well, that's the way he always was. He would smile at you even when he was being a jerk and demanding a huge pay increase. It was impossible to get mad at the guy."

Nevertheless, Holland sided with her vice president. And Mark, who was then being doggedly head-hunted by a number of other agencies because of the high-profile and successful campaigns he led at Alexander, decided to accept an offer from another hi-tech PR firm, Burson-Marsteller. "He came back to me and said, 'You know, I just can't balance in my own head that other people are willing offer me more responsibility and a bigger salary and that I can't get it here. So I think it's time for me to move on.'"

Move on he did. But being one of 2,000 employees at one of Burson-Marsteller's 75 worldwide offices was a far cry from what Mark was used to at Alexander. "The buttoned-up, corporate style was just not a good fit for him," Holland says. Still, Mark handled some exciting clients for B-M, including Sun Microsystems, for whom he helped coordinate the company's sponsorship of the first-ever cybercast lecture series from the White House. But after about a year, he was ready to move on again. In 1998 he accepted a job as communications manager for 3Com Corporation's Mobile Communications Division, where he promoted the company's wireless Internet and hand-held computer technology.

In the few years since he had been at Cal, Mark had made a huge leap into adulthood. Whereas he used to spend hours playing Nintendo or picking his friends' brains over a few beers or during a quick game of one-on-one, he now spent much more than 40 hours a week at work, often bringing his laptop computer home at night. He even took to spending some weeknights at his Uncle Vaughn and Aunt Kathy's home in Saratoga, which was closer to 3Com's Santa Clara headquarters, because he didn't have time to make the commute into San Francisco every night. "Mark may have been born a member of the slacker generation," Paul says, "but he wasn't in any way a part of it." Free time was now a scarce commodity in Mark's life, and when it was available he would most often spend it alone with Paul. That was in sharp contrast with what many of his longtime friends would have preferred. Some of his old-time pals felt that their role in Mark's life had, at this point, been reduced to mobile phone calls during his commute between San Francisco and the Silicon Valley. They say Mark had become a much paler shade of the vibrant friend they'd known just a few years ago.

"There's no question that Paul was the biggest relationship in Mark's life, and you can't take that away," says Dave Kupiecki, who added that he and his wife, Kim, often double-dated with Mark and Paul. Still, he says, it was obvious that Mark's level of interaction with "people outside of his relationship with Paul" took on a different tone. "He was more introverted, he was less spontaneous, and there seemed to be a bit more etiquette in his life than we were used to."

Amanda Mark agrees. "Paul opened Mark's eyes up to a lot of things. And, in fact, Mark wanted to be a lot like Paul—or, with his competitive streak, be more successful than Paul," she says. "But Mark simply didn't see as much of his friends during the period that they were together, and that upset some of us."

As sensitive as he was—and as much as he didn't want to disappoint anyone in his life—Mark recognized the discontent among his friends and was bothered by it. But he understood, as Paul remembers, that this too was a part of the growing-up process. Since joining Alexander, Mark had been on an accelerated career path that was further fueled by the fantastic Internet boom of the middle 1990s. "In addition, he had very important clients and started traveling around a bit and living a bit of the high life as a result," Paul explains. Meanwhile, he says, many of Mark's friends were just graduating from college, beginning to put their adult lives together, and couldn't quite comprehend what Mark was going through. "Mark's friends put him on a pedestal, in a good way. So there was bound to be a bit of friction. There always is when you take away a person who is that important to his group of friends. But Mark loved what he did at work, and he loved what we did together."

In time, however, even Mark started to wonder if he had grown up too fast. Mike McGirr remembers going on a trip to Lake Tahoe with Mark when, in the middle of a late-night soul-searching session, Mark said, "Isn't my life incredible?" and then ended by asking, "I wonder if I'm missing something?"

It wasn't long before that question was crystallizing around his relationship with Paul, Mike says. "He'd say, 'I wonder if I'm doing the right thing by staying in this relationship.'" Invariably, these conversations would end with Mark coming down nine to one in favor of staying in the relationship. Still, that 10% of doubt was enough to keep the question alive. He loved Paul and the time they spent together, and he said that he still yearned to be in a relationship like that of Steven Gold and Bill Hollywood. But now he wondered if he had grabbed for it all a little too early in life. He wasn't even 30 yet. Was he really ready to settle down with one person?

Finally, one day Mark showed up at Mike's house at 1 A.M. "I left Paul," he said. "What do you mean you left? What did you say?" Mike asked. "I didn't say anything," Mark answered. "He was sleeping."

Mark was ready for another chapter in his life but didn't know how Paul would fit into that chapter. And he was afraid to talk with him about it. "He knew he wanted to go out and explore life in a way he couldn't if he was in a monogamous relationship, but at the same time he didn't want to hurt Paul," Mike says. "Mark didn't want to be thought of as the bad guy or as a guy who backed out of a commitment—and that's a good thing. He was just so worried about what people thought about him and had such a strong desire to be loved, accepted, and to not disappoint anyone."

As a result, Paul didn't even know for several days that Mark had left. And when he found out, he was understandably shocked. "Mark always said that it wasn't me and that he just needed to figure out his life," Paul says. "We weren't fighting, and, in fact, we always got along. So I don't think there was any clear reason [for the breakup] other than that."

Still, the breakup—and Paul and Mark's reluctance to fully close the door on the possibility that they would some-day get back together—made it difficult. "On the one hand,

I understood where Mark was coming from. But on the other hand, what can you do when you're in a relationship and there's nothing that can be changed to make it work?" Paul says. "You know, I do believe—and maybe it's too frequently said—that if you love something you have to set it free. And that's what I tried to do with Mark, to see if it was meant to be. So that's where we left it. There was no question that he wanted me in his life—he just needed to figure out where."

"Hey, Mark. It's Mark Wain calling. It's about five minutes to 11 my time, and I just wanted to make sure everything was OK with you. Give me a call back when you get a chance. Talk to you later. Bye."

"Bingham, Petrovich. What's going on? It is that day, that morning, and I'm wondering where the hell you are and hoping to God that you and Amanda are safe—as well as everybody else that we know and love.... Just let me know you're OK, all right? I'll speak to you soon. Bye."

"Mark, it's Corey. I'm just calling to see if you're OK. Give me a call on my cell. Let me know. Bye."

—the 18th, 19th, and 20th unheard voice-mail messages left on Mark Bingham's mobile phone on Sept. 11, 2001— the first from his fraternity brother Mark Wain, the second from his friend Mike Petrovich, and the third from an acquaintance named Corey

MARK HAD MORE THAN A YEAR of experience under his belt at Alexander Communications on Aug. 9, 1995, the day Netscape Communications went public and Wall Street took its first real notice of the hi-tech industry that was blossoming in Northern California. Netscape staged one of the biggest public offerings in history—shares that opened at $28 were selling for more than $70 by the time trading stopped that day. Suddenly a company that gave away its product—an obscure sort of software called a Web browser—and had recorded a $4 million net loss out of $14 million in revenues was worth $2.6 billion.

Startled investors started pouring billions of dollars into other Internet and technology-related companies—overlooking the absence of any proven track record in order to invest in what promised to be the industry of the future. Over the next few years new hi-tech companies opened up across the country, especially in San Francisco, providing these investors with a place to pour their buckets of money. And by 1999 anybody who wasn't already in an Internet-related job was trying to figure out how to get one. In addition, most brick-and-mortar companies that previously had no ties to the Web were scrambling to add some sort of dot-com to their domain.

With his years' worth of a leg up, Mark was well positioned to reap the rewards of this Net boom, as his sizable raises at

Alexander and his subsequent steps up at Burson-Marsteller and 3Com Communications reflected. But by 1999 he too was eager for a bigger piece of the pie and, with all of his experience in hi-tech PR, he started to think about opening his own firm.

Actually, Mark had first started thinking about it years before. Paul Holm remembers that one of his and Mark's frequent dinnertime conversation topics was the future of their respective business lives. "We spent hours and hours talking about everything, including business," says Paul, who had started his own firm, the Holm Group, when he and Mark were still together. "When I was going through some old memorabilia, I found an old menu where, on the back, we had written the potential names for our companies and there was THE BINGHAM GROUP in big letters among all the others." Alice also remembers that Mark had long had dreams of working for himself one day. "He used to tell many of his coworkers at Alexander that he wanted to open his own firm by the time he was 30," she says.

Characteristically, Mark beat his own goal by a year: In early 1999, when he was 29, he quit his job at 3Com and opened The Bingham Group in a San Francisco loft space he shared with a friend's Web-design firm. His first client was eframes.com, a Web site that allowed people to share, store, and print digital photos. In addition, The Bingham Group picked up contract work with 3Com. Soon his company's client roster also included NetSanity, AdFlight, Tenrec, and VARStreet, and by May 2000 he'd hired enough employees that he had to open his own office on San Francisco's Lafayette Street. "At the office-warming party there were probably 200 people, and it took me 20 minutes to get in the door and another 15 minutes to get a spot inside," Alice remembers. "But by that time in my life I had become much more accustomed to having Mark be a larger-than-life figure. He wasn't famous, exactly, but he was extremely popular, and I kind of basked in his reflection."

It was his gregarious nature that, in large part, made The Bingham Group take off. "His professional traits were very much like his personal traits," Ken Montgomery says. "You hear people talk about how he was very much a protector and everyone's best friend. Well, he was like that as a PR professional too. He took all of his accounts very personally, and he was very earnest about each one of them. And that was what made him successful."

In time, the success of The Bingham Group started to afford Mark the opportunity to explore some of the freedom he had been yearning for. He still had to work hard—after all, it was his name on the company. But he was now comfortable enough, financially and emotionally, that he could spend more weeknights away from the office and more weekends kicking back with friends and, for the first time in years, going out as a single man.

After he graduated from Cal, Mark started playing Division I rugby with San Francisco's Olympic Club team, but he had to stop a couple years later after doing severe damage to his ankle during a game. From then on he relegated himself to pickup games of football or basketball, either with friends or with people he'd meet in one of the city's parks. Derrick Mickle was playing in one of those games—a flag football game at Dolores Park—when he first ran head-on into Mark. "Here was this huge guy who was just tearing people up," he says. "And it was kind of frustrating because I had played a lot of pickup football growing up and there was almost an unspoken rule that you didn't showboat." Derrick soon learned that Mark wasn't showing off, but that he just "never dumbed down his game to placate anyone."

Derrick was soon bowled over by Mark's charm too. "He had a personality as big as the sea," he says. And it wasn't long before the two of them started swapping college rugby stories over lunch. Derrick, who played rugby at Vassar College in New York, then tossed the idea of a forming a gay rugby team

Mark's way. When the idea was no more than a "what if," Mark was enthusiastic, he says. But when Derrick got serious, Mark became "dead against" the prospect. "He said, 'You'll never get accepted by the [rugby] union,' 'The guys out there will tear you up,' and 'You won't ever find enough players.'"

Derrick went ahead without Mark's blessing, and just two months after he fielded a "rag-trap of rugby players" for the San Francisco Fog's first practice in October 2000, Mark had a change of heart. "He came out for practice and proceeded to act the same way as when I met him. He just plowed through the field, leaving a sea of bodies," Derrick says, adding that after the team's initial response of "What the hell is this guy doing?" Mark's intensity eventually helped raise the level of everyone's game. And after practice, "Mark's great, nurturing spirit came through," says Bryce Eberhart, who was among those Mark ran over on the field that first day of practice. "He went to everyone and patted them on the back and told them they were doing a great job."

As he had when he first started playing rugby at Los Gatos High School, Mark had again fallen in step with a program that was just right for that point in his life. As a Division III team, the Fog was somewhat less competitive than Mark was used to, which made some allowances for his bum ankle. And for a man who was used to winning, the fact that the Fog never won a game didn't seem to bother him as much as one might expect. "Don't get me wrong, he hated to lose," Derrick says. "But he also understood that there were lessons for us to learn in losing."

As Dave Kupiecki remembers, it wasn't the victories that Mark had missed so much when he wasn't playing rugby—it was the camaraderie. "The thing that he liked about rugby the most was that you went out and you beat the crap out of each other and then you got together and had a barbecue and hung out. That's something unique to the sport of rugby." And with the Fog, unlike the other teams he had played with,

Mark was now hanging out with openly gay team members after the games.

Not everyone on the team was gay, though. One of Derrick's priorities when he founded the Fog was to promote diversity, so they welcomed straight people as well. In fact, Mark's fraternity brother Spencer Kelly, who was one of the people whose reaction Mark was most worried about when he came out to his friends in college, was the first of the team's several straight members.

Still, for Mark, being one of the team's openly gay members was especially significant, as he pointed out in an E-mail in the summer of 2001, when the Fog was accepted as a permanent member of the Northern California Rugby Football Union:

> This is a huge step forward for gay rugby. When I started playing rugby at the age of 16, I always thought that my interest in other guys would be an anathema—completely repulsive to the guys on my team—and to the people I knew I was knocking the shit out of on the other team. I loved the game, but KNEW I would need to keep my sexuality a secret forever. I feared total rejection.
>
> As we worked and sweated and ran and talked together this year, I finally felt accepted as a gay man and a rugby player. My two irreconcilable worlds came together.
>
> Now we've been accepted into the union and the road is going to get harder. We need to work harder. We need to get better. We have the chance to be role models for other gay folks who wanted to play sports, but never felt good enough or strong enough. More importantly, we have the chance to show the other teams in the league that we are as good as they are. Good rugby players. Good partiers. Good sports. Good men.

Gay men weren't always wallflowers waiting on the sideline. We have the opportunity to let these other athletes know that gay men were around all along—on their little league teams, in their class, being their friends.

This is a great opportunity to change a lot of people's minds, and to reach a group that might never have had a chance to know or hear about gay people.

Let's go make some new friends...and win a few games.

Congratulations, my brothers in rugby—

mb

Despite the tone of his E-mail, Mark wasn't becoming a gay activist or even, necessarily, identifying any more as a gay man. He told friends that he considered himself a man of action and that he wanted people to judge him based on those actions. The E-mail to his teammates wasn't a demand for recognition on the rugby field. Mark expected the Fog to earn that recognition just like any other rugby team. But through his E-mail he acknowledged a number of things: First, Derrick was right all along; second, the closet didn't have to be as much a fact of life as he had thought; and third, he could make things better for himself and others by being more open about his sexual orientation. Still, as Amanda points out, "He never really did anything actively to promote the gay community apart from the fact that he would challenge people's ideas about what it meant to be gay." And, as far as he was now concerned, a gay rugby team could be the perfect challenge.

Still, Mark's definition of what it meant to be gay of course differed from other people's definitions. As much as he identified with the hypermasculinity of the bear scene and the just-a-guy appeal of the gay sports scene, he sometimes had a negative reaction to and was critical of people who identified with the opposite end of the spectrum—"real effeminate gays," as he described them in his letter to Mark Wilhelm when he was 19. He was hardly alone in this feeling. In fact, if 10 gay men were asked to describe a gay pride parade, at least seven of them would likely make a disparaging comment about the "nelly guys in spandex" or the "queens with the feather boas." Popularity should never make a wrong opinion right, but because Mark's criticisms of effeminate gay men are so often heard from others as well, they are more likely a reflection of a broader difficulty gay people have dealing with stereotypes in general than they are of any specific dislike Mark had for effeminate gay men. Stereotypes become stereotypes because they do apply to some people. Mark just wasn't one of those people.

"To some degree, to say that Mark was *gay* gay is almost a misnomer. He accepted that he was attracted to men, but so much of the scene, what we know as gay life, didn't appeal to him. It just wasn't his style," Derrick says. "But Mark wasn't straight-acting either. He was just acting like Mark. Sure, your gaydar would hit zero every time you saw him, but you would be so wrong."

Mark was definitely still hitting the gay bar scene, sometimes with his new friends from the team, other times with his older friends, including his fraternity brothers, and still other times with a mix of them all. Some of his more muscular fraternity brothers sometimes even helped Mark meet men by taking off their shirts at these clubs and then introducing Mark to the men they attracted.

But by the end of October 1999 Mark found himself in his third and last long-term relationship, with 24-year-old Joe Cinquini. He and Joe had met on the Internet in the summer of 1996, but because Mark was dating Paul at the time, Joe says he and Mark were only friends then—sometimes getting together for a few beers or to watch a game of basketball. "He was talking about wanting to move to New York back then," Joe says. "And when we lost touch after a while I kind of assumed he had moved." Then out of the blue, three years later, Joe got a message from Mark on his answering machine. "He said, 'Hey Joey, this is Mark Bingham. We're going to go play basketball tonight, and I wanted to know if you wanted to come down.'" Joe was almost as surprised to hear from Mark as Mark was to hear back from Joe. "It turned out that he hadn't meant to call me at all," Joe explains. "He was trying to reach another of his friends who played hoops with him."

Nevertheless, they got together again, and then, at the end of October, Joe and a girlfriend of his attended Mark's Halloween party where they got "pretty liquored up in the Bingham style," Joe says. Because Joe lived outside of San Francisco, Mark offered to sleep on the couch so Joe and his friend could sleep in his bed. "Mark, being the guy that he was, though, had a plan," Joe says. "I went to the couch to cover him with a blanket and say good-night and he said, 'What, no good night kiss?' And when I said, 'No, no kiss,' he grabbed me and we kissed for the first time. And that's how the Joey and Mark relationship got going."

From the beginning Mark told Joe that he wasn't the type of guy to settle down and that he was kind of like his mother—always on the go because of his career. His actions, however, indicated the opposite. While they maintained separate homes, Mark and Joe were always together—either at Joe's home in Belmont, which is about 20 minutes outside of San Francisco, or at Mark's apartment in the city. And when they weren't sharing a sushi dinner or dim sum at a downtown restaurant, they were often hanging out with each other's families. Christmas was spent with Joe's family and New Year's with Mark's. "It was like we had been together for 10 years, but we were just really comfortable," Joe says. "I remember watching him sit there with my father watching football and I would just crack up and say, 'Oh my God, this is insane.' "

In September, Mark headed to the Olympic Games, which were being held in Amanda's hometown of Sydney. Together with Amanda and her parents, Mark attended a "heap of events," Amanda remembers, including a basketball game between the United States and Lithuania, the triathlon, and an equestrian competition, where they sat so close they ended up covered in mud and horse blood. "Mark, of course, was thrilled," says Amanda. But by far his favorite Olympic attraction was the torch relay. "Every time the torch was run somewhere in the city Mark went to see it," she says, estimating that Mark saw the torch relay at least three different times. "One day he got especially excited when he was watching the flame on Oxford Street [in Sydney's gay district] and all these drag queens showed up in their torch outfits. He thought that was great."

Just weeks after the Olympic Games ended, Amanda moved to New York City, as she had been planning to do for a few years. In fact, when Amanda first talked about the move two years earlier, Mark said he would go with her. "I was on vacation in the city and Mark was there for work, and we were in a cab going down Fifth Avenue when we decided we had to move there," Amanda says. But Mark couldn't have anticipated the success of The Bingham Group in 1998, and two years later, when Amanda got the job transfer she had been waiting for with her employer, Morgan Stanley, Mark told her he had to stay in San Francisco. "I told him that I understood and that I didn't expect him to be able to move when I could," she says. "But I did expect him to make frequent visits."

Amanda wasn't too surprised that within a month of her move Mark called to say he was coming out. After all, she'd been telling him about all the wonderful things she'd been doing since moving—walks in Central Park, drinks in the

Village, and movies on 42nd Street. Of course he was eager to visit. But when she said, "Great, when are you visiting?" Mark answered, "No, I'm moving to New York."

Business was going so well at The Bingham Group the fall of 2000 that the firm could basically pick and choose the clients it wanted to work with. And Mark realized he could look at this windfall in two ways. The first was to assume, as he had been, that he should stay in San Francisco in order to direct the company through this and on to future successes. The second was to simply enjoy his company's success while it lasted. He had disposable income and he was his own boss. When, if ever, would there be a better opportunity to pick up and move to New York City to live with one of his best friends?

The decision wasn't a tough one from a business standpoint. "He loved the idea that he was president of his own company. It wasn't a vanity thing, but it was a sign that he had arrived," Ken Montgomery says. "But he didn't like the day-to-day running of a business. I remember distinctly, when he first started The Bingham Group, that he would get frustrated about having to go from meeting to meeting or having to deal with personnel issues. I knew then that this wasn't really what he wanted to do."

It was more difficult on a personal front, though. Before Mark had left for Sydney, Joe had sold his home in Belmont and he and Mark were considering getting a place together. But their relationship started to get tense when Mark got back from Sydney. "I could tell there was something on his mind when were house hunting," Joe says, "and the tension kind of boiled over one day when we were moving some furniture out of my house. Mark said something to me and took my comeback like I meant it smart or something, and he said, 'Fuck you.' I looked at him and said, 'Say that again and I'll never give you another chance to say it.' And he just looked at me and said, 'Fuck you.' "

The two of them officially called it quits a few days later, and like he did when they'd first met in 1996, Mark told Joe about his plan to move to New York City with Amanda. "He said, 'I hope when I come back I can still sweep you off your feet,' " Joe recalls. "And I, being the asshole I am, said, 'Good luck. I'm not going to make it easy.' Mark wanted to live the jet-setter life. But I think, more importantly, he was worried about committing. He was worried about settling down and ending up old and fat with kids."

When Mark told Alice about his intention to move, she was crestfallen. "But by this point I knew better than anyone not to try to talk Mark out of anything," she says.

Mark's plan was to be bicoastal. He was going to spend three weeks in New York running what were to become the New York offices of The Bingham Group, and then he'd return to San Francisco for the following three weeks before starting the cycle again. And that was still the plan when he moved to New York and, in March 2001, announced the opening of his New York office. But in the time between his decision to move to the East Coast and the date of his actual move, the bottom fell out of the hi-tech market just as quickly as it had exploded six years earlier.

The Bingham Group, like most other companies in San Francisco and the Silicon Valley, started losing business. And for the first time since Damon Billian had taught him to punch in middle school, Mark didn't fight back. Whether it was a conscious decision or not, he drifted further away from his eponymous company, choosing to spend less time in the office and more time simply enjoying the money that he had saved, which, for the time being, was still coming in.

Not that he was a complete sloth when he was in New York City. He did make several unsuccessful attempts to secure clients in the city, and he still conducted some business for the San Francisco office—although that only required that he get up by noon New York time and, since he was usually working in the living room of his and Amanda's Chelsea apartment, meant he didn't even have to get dressed if he didn't want to.

In fact, he often worked in his underwear, Amanda says. With all the restaurants, museums, and bars in the city— Mark was especially fond of the bar Hogs and Heifers, which was made popular by the movie *Coyote Ugly*—and with the 17 sets of guests he and Amanda hosted their first nine months in the city, there was plenty to keep Mark occupied when he wasn't working.

And in case he started to miss home, he could go stay with Steven Gold and Bill Hollywood, who lived only a train ride away, in Shorthills, N.J. "He'd come down here and stay for the weekend," Bill says. "And on Sunday mornings, when Steven would get up to make waffles, Mark would come into our room and fight over the remote with me. I always wanted to watch *CBS Sunday Morning*, but as soon as I'd set the remote down he would put the TV on ESPN."

By summer, Mark was taking a break even from New York City, spending a couple weekends at Fire Island with Steven and Bill at their friend Stan Moldovan's place and jetting off to Italy for a business trip that became more of a vacation.

It was clear that the hi-tech "downturn," as it was being called, was significantly more serious than the word "downturn" could ever suggest. Most of Mark's former colleagues—including Holland Carney and Ken Montgomery—were making significant career changes, in part in response to the souring economy. Mark knew he too would have to make some big decisions regarding his company and his professional future. Whether in response to the looming changes in his life or not, in July he did what his grandmother and mother had done when they were his age and found themselves in similar states of transition—he turned to literature for inspiration. But where his grandmother had turned to Willard Price and *The Amazing Amazon* and his mother had turned to John Steinbeck and *Cannery Row*, Mark turned to Ernest Hemingway and *The Sun Also Rises*.

Hemingway's first novel, it tells the story of a group of English and American expatriates who journey from Paris's Left Bank to

Pamplona, Spain, for the seven-day San Fermin festival, which includes the running of the bulls and ensuing bullfights. It was Spencer Kelly who first suggested they make the trip. "I knew Mark was screwing around a lot at that point, and I thought Pamplona was a natural for him," he says. "He was such a bruiser, and he was always open to putting himself in harm's way. I think he saw some valor in bleeding, actually. That's the way he played rugby, and that's the way he lived life: Dive in headfirst, and if you got skinned up on the bottom, then so be it."

Certainly, if Hemingway's description of the festival is to be believed, it was a perfect fit for Mark:

There were so many people running ahead of the bulls that the mass thickened and slowed up going through the gate into the ring, and as the bulls passed, galloping together, heavy, muddy-sided, horns swinging, one shot ahead, caught a man in the running crowd in the back and lifted him in the air. Both the man's arms were by his sides, his head went back as the horn went in, and the bull lifted him and then dropped him. The bull picked up another man running in front, but the man disappeared into the crowd, and the crowd was through the gate and into the ring with the bulls behind them. The red door of the ring went shut, the crowd on the outside balconies of the bull-ring were pressing through to the inside, there was a shout, then another shout.

The man who had been gored lay face down in the trampled mud. People climbed over the fence, and I could not see the man because the crowd was so thick around him. From inside the ring came the shouts. Each shout meant a charge by some bull into the crowd. You could tell by the degree of intensity in the shout how bad a thing it was that was happening. Then the rocket went up that meant the steers had gotten the bulls out of the ring and into the corrals. I left the fence and started back toward the town.

Unlike Jake Barnes and the other characters in Hemingway's book, Mark and his friends began their trek from London rather than Paris. But otherwise the trip was pretty close to what Papa had scripted, right down to the late, alcohol-filled nights, the friends lost and found in the crowd, and the eruption of cheers when the bulls got the better of them.

The group lost Jason Escamilla when they were in Madrid— he got too drunk, thought he was still in London, and kept asking the cab driver to take him to the Hotel Russell, where they'd stayed in London. And they couldn't find Mark or Rob Anderson the Thursday morning they were all supposed to run with the bulls. So once the second rocket went off that morning, indicating that the bulls had been released, the actual running seemed rather uneventful in comparison. "It was the mildest of the seven days," Spencer says. "Nobody was killed, and I don't think anybody even got seriously injured."

Mark found Spencer and Jason just as the bulls were being released, and the three of them successfully ran with them through the streets and into the bull arena without being touched. Mark immediately sent an E-mail letting everyone know that they had made it to Pamplona and had made it through the festival unscathed. "I was especially relieved to get that E-mail on the 14th of July that said they were all OK," says Alice, who had heard horror stories about American tourists being gored in Pamplona. "Then the next day, I got another E-mail...."

Subject: Umm...we decided to run with the bulls again...
Date: Sun, 15 Jul 2001
From: Mark Bingham

So I know I sent some of you the E-mail about how we ran safely in the "Encierro" (the running of the bulls) in

Pamplona. Well...that was on Thursday, July 12.

Basically, Rob, one of the four guys and two girls with us...kind of never made it home on Wed. night and missed the running at 8 a.m. Thursday...so Rob, Jay, and I had to come back and run again on Saturday morning, July 14—the final day of the Festival de San Fermin...our last chance.

THIS time, not only did we actually run next to and touch the bulls in the street...we ran into the Plaza de Toros for the craziness that follows—this is basically 30 minutes of drunk amateurs "playing" with the "small" bulls in the Bull Ring after the 1,200-pound bulls run through the streets.

They release the bulls one by one from a corridor...six bulls total...into the arena...where a crowd of about 100 crazy men taunt and harass the bulls...then dodge as the bull careens around the ring. The good news is, the bulls are smaller and they have their horns taped and/or cut short. The bad news is, both Rob and I got gored...well, more like hit head-on by the bull and knocked to the ground.

We saw this happening repeatedly to other people too, much to the delight of the crowd. The arena is PACKED with people...all waiting to see the bulls chase people and roaring their approval when the bull actually gets a hold of someone.

Most folks dodge the bull...or jump over the five-foot wall encircling the ring. In my case, I got hit by the bull from the right side...and the horns were on either side of me, and he butted me with his head and I rode along with him for a few feet...I tried to push off with my hands, but I got knocked to the floor. The crowd began to roar. It's wild when you realize that 15,000 people are bellowing and whistling in unison...as they watch you get tossed by a 600-pound animal. The potential for injury and death drives them into a frenzy.

Anyway...at this point, you're supposed to cover your head and lie flat on the dirt, covering your face. (Interestingly, what's on the ground doesn't seem to interest the bulls much.)

When the bull is on top of you...the crowd closes in to help...they yank the bull's tail and wave newspapers to distract the bull from the prone/gored person. My bull stomped on me a couple times, and then ran off to gore someone else.

I got up, dusted off, and a bunch of people ran up and said, "Dude! That was awesome!" and "Hey, your hat didn't come off!" There were lots of high fives with random people from every country. I realized that my leg was bloody...and worse, my right side was covered with bull poop.

Then a diminutive long-haired Spanish guy walked up and asked me for a cigarette. He seemed pretty blase about the whole thing.

Jay got nicked and chased by a different bull...and Rob, well...wayward Rob got the same treatment I got.

So we've all got our bruises, cuts, and scrapes, but we're doing great. We adjourned promptly to the Cafe Iruna (made famous by Hemingway in *The Sun Also Rises*) and ordered four beers and a pitcher of sangria...it was 8:40 A.M.

I've got many more stories to tell...but they'll have to wait until I'm back. This trip has been TOTALLY amazing.

Bonus: Spain is pretty cheap too.

We're off to Bordeaux tomorrow, we're staying in a chateau...and doing some wine tasting...which promises to be more serene than the last few days.

I'll try to write more soon.

mb

Mark provided further details about the trip, as well as about some of his other summer activities, in an E-mail he wrote to Ken Montgomery, who had just left his job in the Silicon Valley to work for nine months as a volunteer teacher at an orphanage in the African country of Malawi:

Bonjour Ken!

Comment ca vas? It's Mark. I JUST got in from Paris. Literally, I walked in the door just a few minutes ago. We had the most amazing, exhilarating, wild time in Europe. I've got lots to tell you, but first comments on your E-mail:

WOW!

It sounds like you are really helping improve people's lives. That must be the most incredible feeling! I'm thinking about you a lot. I miss working out, talking about sports, our inside jokes and all the uncontrollable laughter we derive from dishing on the queens here in S.F. (I haven't been back here since mid-May!!)

So what kind of actual food is it...local fare? Or like burgers and stuff. Also, I don't understand the part about the cook...he came from Mozambique JUST to cook for you?? That can't be right.

So what can we do over here to help...cash donations, send Nikes, send pictures from Italy and France for your geography sessions?

I WOULD LOVE to teach kids...that must be a blast.

So I've been traveling for a couple of months now...you heard about my high jinks in Italy. That was a BLAST...so sorry I haven't scanned photos yet...just lots of frantic travel happening. I'll try to do it next week.

I came back to N.Y. for a few days between June 25 and 4th of July... Lots of fun stuff there: went to Fire Island for a gorgeous weekend, saw the Macy's 4th of July fireworks with Amanda and Mike Petrovich from a friend's rooftop apartment on the East River...It was like our OWN PERSONAL FIREWORKS SHOW. There were throngs of people—hundreds of thousands—lining the waterfront... and we were 15 stories up...eating canapes in this guy's apartment, drinking champagne, and then scampering up to the roof for the pyrotechnics...very cool.

Andrew Smith and Kobren and a couple of other guys came to N.Y. to play this wacky basketball tournament...I couldn't play as I was still nursing my dislocated shoulder from the D.C. rugby tourney.

Anyway, I bailed for London to meet Spencer Kelly and Jay and some other friends on July 5th. The afternoon I left, my cop friend in N.Y. came over and then he drove me to the airport before the trip.... He used the siren and lights to get us through traffic...heh heh...

London was a blast. Didn't do much shopping...so pricey, but we partied a lot...did the club scene...and enjoyed London much more than prior visits because my friend Rob lives there now and knows the scene.

Went to Tower of London/Crown Jewels. Tate Museum and new Tate Modern Addition, National Gallery. The food basically sucked (the guys I was with were a bit on a budget, so we weren't going upscale). In general, we lived pretty cheap the whole trip...three, four, sometimes five in a room.

Flew to Madrid—what an awesome city! Then caught a train to Pamplona. I cannot tell you how wild Pamplona was... I'd just read *The Sun Also Rises*...and Hemingway's prep for this event was so on-target...and the book is 60 years old!

Anyway, I think I copied you on the E-mail, but we survived the running...but I wound up getting gored and run over by a bull in the bullring after the run! (If I haven't sent you the detailed description E-mail...let me know and I'll resend.)

After the drunken festival atmosphere of Pamplona, we moved out to the coast to San Sebastian...just gorgeous...If you get a chance to take a week off in Europe...go to San Sebastian, very cool. Ibiza is supposed to be cool too...haven't been, but I'm itching to go back to Spain.

France was much more mellow and upscale...lots of great wine! Bordeaux region...then Sauterne for the sweet wines, and then six days in Paris...totally decompressing, having fine wines and majestic prix fixe meals. It was awesome.

I'm worried that I sound like an asshole talking about this lavishness while you are dealing with grinding poverty in Africa...my apologies.

Anyway, it's nice to be back in San Francisco today...of course, it's like 90 degrees on the peninsula...and 50 degrees and foggy at my apartment.

I have no car, no cell phone, no laptop, because I forgot that my return flight from Europe was nonstop to S.F....all my shit is in N.Y.!!

Oh well...I can DEFINITELY make do. I'm not in ANY mood to work...I'll get my car tomorrow...my mom is picking me up in S.F. tonight.

So, Ken, overall life is good. I'm anxious to hear more about your Malawi...I thought there would be LOTS more kids there...like hundreds. How many kids are in your orphanage? Do you have your own room? Are you safe? Is security an issue at all? I hear about kidnappings of Westerners...and just general ethnic strife among rival factions in Africa.

Also: lame question—is there any possibility of dating anybody from nearby towns...you must be busting at the seams...

Okey doke...I'm jet-lagged. Gotta gotta get some snooze time in.

I'm going on a fitness jag soon...gonna get BIG!

Your Cal Bear Brother,

Mark

What Mark didn't describe in either E-mail was the souvenir of a scar he came home with. The horseshoe-shaped wound on the back of his left leg was actually infected by the time he and his friends made it to Bordeaux. "His toe started getting numb, and the wound was getting all festery," Spencer says. "Then I looked it up on the Internet and realized that he probably had tetanus." Mark spent the rest of the trip on antibiotics. But once it healed, he was left with a definite badge of courage. "Short of having a gore wound right through the belly or across the chest, he had the best excuse for telling people what he'd done," Spencer says. "When someone asked him, 'Whoa, where did that come from?' he could say, 'Ah, that's from when I ran with the bulls.' It was proof that he really lived." Or, as Hemingway would have said, proof that Mark was an aficionado.

"Hey, Mark. It's Jason. Just trying to get a hold of you to make sure you and Amanda are OK. Give me a call back. Talk to you later. Bye."

"Hey, Mark. This is Mary, Damon's mom. Just trying to check up and to make sure that you and Amanda are OK. If you have a chance try to give Damon a call because he's a little concerned. I hope all is well with you and you were nowhere near the tragedy today. I'll talk to you later. Bye-bye, sweetie."

"Hey, Mark. It's Joe. I just want to make sure you're OK. If you could drop me a line and let me know, it would be great.... So if you could give me a call I would greatly appreciate it. Bye-bye.

—the 20th, 21st, and 22nd unheard voice-mail messages left on Mark Bingham's mobile phone on Sept. 11, 2001— the first from his fraternity brother Jason Escamilla; the second from Damon Billian's mother, Mary Billian; and the third from his ex-boyfriend Joe Cinquini

"BEFORE MARK LEFT FOR SPAIN, HE mentioned that when he got back to the States it would be time for pre-season football," Bill Hollywood says. Just as Mark's long E-mails in July served as such a vivid travelogue of his trip to Europe that month, this much shorter E-mail shows what was clearly on his mind when he got back home:

Subject: Dolphins Schedule, my schedule
Date: Mon, 13 Aug 2001
From: Mark Bingham

Hi all,

So the fins have a preseason game tonight, Monday at 5 p.m. against the Bucs on ESPN. Might be fun to watch the first half...I'm sure the rest will be a real garbage dump. Why didn't we ditch Jay Fielder and get a real quarterback?! Anyway, the exact 2001 schedule is here: http://www.dol-fantalk.com/_dolphins_stuff/schedule.shtml.

Please note the 12-16-01 matchup with the niners at Candlestick!! Should we try to get GOOD seats??? Tailgating December 16 is probably a bad call though....

I'm planning to attend one or two of the games against the Jets and/or Buffalo when I'm in New York. Also, check out the Miami Herald's football page now and then: http://www.miami.com/herald/content/sports/football

FYI on my schedule:

S.F. through Aug. 23
Vegas Aug. 24-26
N.Y. Aug. 25-Sept. 13
S.F. Sept. 13-24 (two weddings consecutive weekends)
N.Y. Sept. 23-Oct. 12
Potentially Iowa and Michigan football games (Oct. 13 Michigan, Oct. 20 Iowa-Indiana in Iowa City) and visit Josh
S.F. Oct. 22-Nov. 19 (Shrader Halloween party 10/27 and Big Game at Stanford 11/17)
N.Y. Nov. 18-Dec. 15 (Thanksgiving etc.)
S.F. Dec. 16-TBD (Niners-Dolphins, Christmas etc.)

Who wants to come out and visit in New York???

Football and the Miami Dolphins had been around for every one of the 32 fall seasons that Mark had been alive. The enthusiasm he expressed in his E-mail was automatic for him by now. It was as much a part of autumn for him as were the sun in the southern sky and the chill in the air. But this season was more foreboding for him than most for a number of reasons—not the least of which was the fact that, after months of having more carefree fun than he'd had in years, he knew it was time to get serious again. He wondered how much longer he could realistically expect himself to be able to live on two coasts. If he had to choose between San Francisco and New York, how could he? He was tired of dating and asked himself if he would ever meet the right guy again. And if he did, could he allow himself to settle down?

But probably most pressing was his concern for his business. The economy was showing no signs of improving for the hi-tech industry, and The Bingham Group's client roster had dropped from six full-time clients to two. Clearly, things were going to have to change. But how?

As he had his whole life, Mark turned to his closest friends for advice as he pondered these and other questions about his future. For some of his friends, this was the last time they talked with Mark. And for Ken Montgomery, who was still volunteering at an orphanage in Malawi, the conversation was recorded in an E-mail he received from Mark in August. (Ken's comments are in italics, Mark's in plain text.)

Hi Ken,

So good to get your E-mail. I was feeling a little blue, and reading about your exploits and touching experiences with the kids definitely gave me some perspective. I'll try to embed some responses to your E-mail below...and then I'll write more at the bottom.

Once again this is long, so grab a cup of coffee. Let me know if you would prefer shorter E-mails, if ones this long are just too hard to read.

The longer the better. I'm serious, these read like a memoir or a novel. You need to make sure: 1) that you save all of your correspondence during this trip, and 2) that you keep a diary. You should publish it one day...seriously. If not for a mass market audience, then at least for yourself. I'm sure that you would love to have all of these notes, E-mails, photos, and letters in one place so you can peruse it all 10, 20, 50 years from now.

So nice to finally hear from you!!! Sounds like you had a great time "on the continent" and in London. I love London and was just writing my friend Jaime how much I miss jetting off there to just hang out and go shopping. You were there for Harrods' big sale, you should have gone to that. That is where I bought a ton of stuff last year so inexpensively. I think I mentioned to you that I went to the Tate Modern last November. I love how they converted the power plant and the art, well it was interesting. I also liked all the new underground stops, very cool. I hope that with this new economy it doesn't mean that we have to give up things like that...life is so much more fun when you get to do all that!

I had the best time in London that I've ever had. I've been there before, but by myself...and I didn't know what to do. This time we were with a group...and hanging out with some folks who live there, so I really enjoyed it. I'm so bad. I really should have focused more on the cultural experience of it, but I was with two friends from Cal, so we did a lot of partying...and sleeping in till noon.

Missed the sale. I need to cut costs right now anyway. More on that later.

Pamplona sounds awesome. Glad to hear it lived up to your expectations. I have thought about doing that but frankly thought it would be kind of Disney-ified if you know what I mean. On what part of your body did you get gored? I wouldn't want you to be too much like Jake in The Sun Also Rises! *I did not get the E-mail you sent out (thanks for thinking of me—I guess I know where I stand that I don't even merit a group-mail inclusion...) but I would love to hear about it.*

It was so not Disney-fied. We kept saying how you should have been there. It's funny because I didn't know what to expect, but I was sure that the uniqueness and human drama of the San Fermin Festival would be eroded by the gawking, plastic, touristy masses, but it wasn't. It was a drunk-fest, just as Hemingway described it. And, yeah, lots of tourists, but so were we. And we just got caught up in it. If I were in a different mindset, older perhaps, and not interested in partaking, just watching—then it would have sucked. But we knew we were going to run in the Encierro. We knew we could get hurt. We know it was all about consuming mass quantities of sangria, dancing until all hours, and sleeping in the park. It was just a blast!

I was always on the lookout for handsome guys. We spent hours at the Cafe Iruna, relating our stories, talking about the morning's run, being the confidant of others on the trip...but then blurting out everything we heard to other people on the trip. In many respects, our visit to Spain was much like the one Hemingway described. Four guys with distinct personalities, a couple of girls. New friends coming and going. We never even got into a fight over three weeks. Pretty surprising.

If you're gonna do it...I recommend doing it with a group of people.

I would also love to go to Ibiza but I would NOT want to go looking like I do. I definitely think one needs to be in prime shape for that kind of event! Ryan went there a couple of years ago and said he had a blast. I was in Mykonos a few years ago (which is supposed to be something like Ibiza) and had a really good time, though I really didn't do any of the clubbing stuff at all. Just hung out at the beach, ate well and slept and slept some more. I think that is about the most relaxed I've ever been.

I can't wait to go back to Spain, Ibiza or wherever. You know what's weird? I feel like I have a biological clock ticking. I mean, we're only young and able to get exactly what we want sexually for a relatively limited window of time...I know that's kind of morbid. But realistically, 16-35 you can pretty much get whatever you want. And then the gut arrives, and the hair goes, and then—even mentally— we start to not be able to play the game as well. It's all so new when you're a wide-eyed 20-something, but I find myself going through the motions now. I can't articulate exactly what I mean....

I mean: now when I meet people, I don't feel that anticipation of wondering "Is this the one?"...and worse, I don't even feel like I want to be in a relationship, where before I definitely wanted to find the RIGHT GUY for a relationship. Anyway, boring topic. But I'm a little over the dating thing right now. Dario in Italy was a welcome change, he was so earnest. But the guys in Paris...and here in the states...BLECH. Your famous Folsom Street wretch...speaking of that...went to Dore Alley with some guys from the rugby team two days after I flew in from CDG... What a bunch of lame-ass, hairy, droopy, saggy faggots in tight clothes. PLEASE don't let that be me someday! Please please please. I left after about one hour. Some enormous fat guy with a cottage-cheese ass and faux angel wings and a Viking helmet was being bent over to get paddled at the spanking booth...and THAT was my cue to leave.

I went home and ate a pint of Ben & Jerry's and watched golf...pathetic!

The 4th of July in New York sounds great. I spent a 4th there about 10 years ago and we watched the fireworks from the Brooklyn Bridge. It was pretty amazing and unlike San Francisco, no fog! So how was Fire Island? Tell me about it. Did it live up to your expectations?

Fire Island sucks, dude. The answer is no. Too many steroided-up gym queens, bad Chelsea attitude and this nasty sense that you "owe" people because you dropped by their house for a cocktail. I just didn't like it much. My other friends have a boat though...and we had a good time partying on the boat...they are down-to-earth, sports-minded guys and we had a nice time dishing on the queens.

So I take it you have not been able to sell your car yet? Are you still trying? I know we say this over and over but it is just so amazing what a difference a year makes. So how is your business going? I received an E-mail from Jeff Davis, who said his is pretty much in the crapper (his words) and that unless something miraculous happens he will probably have to close shop. That is really too bad to hear.

No, I still have the car...have had a couple of people look at it, but not a lot of bites. YES, the downturn is exactly to blame...there's a glut of luxury trucks on the market right now.

The business is doing better than some I guess...we're making a LITTLE money (I'm netting a few $K per month). I actually feel good about things. We have a stable client or two...and I needed a break so I traveled for two months. The business continued to make money while I was out fucking around. That was awesome. Here's what I'm thinking about now though: If I fired one of my staff, that $6K a month would go directly in my pocket. I want to move to a smaller space to lower our rent, and then I'll be making decent money.

The catch: I have to start working again! This is my main problem...I haven't worked hard in eight months or so. I've been loafing. I've got cash saved, which is good. But if I worked, just a little even, I'd be making some fat cash.
I guess I'm ready to begin working again...no worries.

I got a nice E-mail from Sheldon, who said that most of the VC's [venture capitalists] in the Valley don't see things improving until later in 2002 at the earliest. But then they didn't see all this happening, so who really knows. I just hope when I decide to come back there will be a job for me. I have told a couple people that maybe I was foolish to turn down jobs when I had the chance, but I don't really think that and really believe that I am doing the right thing for me.

Dude, just reading your E-mails, I can tell you made a great decision. I wish I was doing it too. You will NEVER regret volunteering your time and your life the way you are now.

So on to what is going on here... To answer some of your questions, the food is actually very good. Lots and lots of fish, which comes right out of the lake. It is very good. Lots of vegetables and rice, as you would expect. Also eat chicken fairly regularly. The thing that locals eat, as have I, is sima, which is made from cornflower and boiled, and you eat it out of a communal bowl with relishes and other stuff. It is actually pretty good. So the cook is from Mozambique, now living in Malawi. He only works for me. Frankly it feels a little ridiculous to have my own personal valet in a third-world country, but it gives him a job.

He gets paid a whopping K2000 (the K is for "kwacha") a month, which at current rates translates into about $30. But that is actually not bad for this part of the world. I just about made his year last week when I surprised him and bought him a bicycle. There are so many bikes here, it is like China. But you know how every big American car made in the '50s seems to have made its way to Cuba? That's what it is like for bicycles here. Anyway, the bike cost about $35 but as you can imagine that would have been hard for him so I took care of it. That way he does not have to continue walking the five kilometers (three miles) to get here.

So the orphanage is not something like you would see in Annie. *The basic goal of Malawi Children's Village is to enable the children with some independence. We get the very young children in here. Right now we have six—and they are placed back into the village, into a surrogate home, when they are about 2. Each village has two volunteers who are conduits for MCV and who take care of problems and issues there. If there is something they cannot handle then the people come here. Every morning from 8:00 a.m. to noon people are able to drop in for medical help. I have to say I really don't like going in the center at that time because some of these people just look so sad and some have gashes here and there, but that is part of life here.*

Nice of you to buy him a bike. It's so funny to think that what we leave as a tip in a fine restaurant ($30)...can pay a good month's salary for someone in Malawi. I just bought a $90 bottle of wine. Christ!

The way you said "gashes," it sounds like there is something specific to be afraid of. Are there other weird diseases and parasites that you're worried about? The one that really scares me is the Ebola virus. It's like airborne by saliva and deadly within days and there's no cure. That is some scary shit. I read an article about the Africa outbreaks in *The New York Times Magazine*. Grrrreat...let's get Ken wound up about African diseases!!

I do have my own room that is perfectly nice. I have a full bed (I do miss my new king bed with all that great bedding, not to sound too gay...). I have attached a picture of it. If this did not suit me, like I mentioned to you before there are actually some ridiculously nice resorts right by the lake—just part of the dichotomy between the haves and have-nots in third-world countries.

Crime here is absolutely minimal, especially given that it is a third-world country, actually more like fifth-world.... Crime is simply

not a part of their culture and is severely frowned upon. There apparently is a growing tendency for young children to approach you for money, but it is telling that older kids, my students who are about 18, 19, really intensely dislike this. It is harmless and all, and they don't know better, but it is annoying at times. They are basically asking for a kwacha, which as I said is about 1.3 cents.... As far as kidnapping goes, I don't think I have heard of that very much at all in Africa, unlike Southeast Asia and the Pacific. I think the Philippines. Not to say I am planning any trips to Sierra Leone or to Libya any time soon. I am planning on driving to Mozambique and then from there hopping on a flight to Madagascar, which is supposed to be amazing. I would also like to go to Senegal (did I tell you I met the president?) and a few other places. I figure I should be able to take some weeklong trips while I am here. As for the rival factions thing, that is definitely true in some countries. You just have to avoid those places, again like Sierra Leone.

As far as the chance of meeting some guys here, that is not going to happen. First off, I don't think homosexuality is real popular here. It might not even be legal, I'm not sure about that. Of course the funny thing is that men will walk down the street hand in hand. They are just a very warm and friendly culture. But secondly and more importantly, Mark, this is an AIDS-ravaged third-world country where hygiene is not an everyday (or every week) issue and I just can't fathom anything happening (I say trying to not do a Folsom Street wretch). There are so many sweet people though that you just want to give a hug. Back to the above, seriously, people simply do not bathe regularly here. They don't have plumbing, after all. So at first the natural body smell kind of gets to you. But eventually you get used to it and there is almost something endearing about it. I know that sounds weird and I really can't put that thought into words, but it's just who they are.

Yes, that sounds weird.

So Mark, I love what I'm doing with the students. I have thoroughly enjoyed them all. They have really opened up with me and we have a lot of fun. I took them all to one of the hotels on the lake last week to go swimming and for most of them it was the first time they have been in a pool. We had a lot of fun. The best part for me was a few of them challenged me to a race across the pool (a fairly long pool) and I beat them, thus solidifying my "cool" factor with them. There had been much bravado before about what great swimmers they were, so it was actually quite sweet to see their deference, though I have to say if they would have used proper techniques they would have blown me out of the water, they are after all 15 years (ouch, that hurts to say) younger than I am. But I will let someone else in the future take care of showing them that!

Two Saturdays ago I took them all to Blantyre for the Malawi-South African soccer match. It was the first time several of them had been to Blantyre (it is about three hours south of here) and the first time any of them had been to a soccer match. They were so excited and had a great time. I was starved and wanted something good so I took them to brunch at the l'Meridien in Blantyre and it was so cool because the South African soccer team was having lunch in there. The captain of the team and a couple of the players came over and said hi and took pictures with us. The captain in particular was positively charming and such a gracious person. As you know, soccer is huge here and so this would be like Derek Jeter or Michael Jordan saying hi to kids in the states. They were all so thrilled. Plus later that day at the game, Malawi beat S.A. in something of an upset, so it was just about a perfect day for them. Two days ago I took them back to their boarding school (holiday is over) and even though it is about 30 miles, the drive took about two hours over some of the worst "roads" I have ever traversed. But it was great seeing their boarding school and it was also very sweet because they all took the time to thank me for everything I had done for them, they told me they had seen stuff they never thought they would see and that they would remember it all until their grave. It honestly almost made me cry. I just told them sincerely that the pleasure was all mine. I then told them that if I decided to drive to Mozambique that maybe I would stop in to see them. One of them said he didn't like the "maybe" part—just like kids in the U.S.! I told them that for sure I would stop in to see them and if not then I would be in Malawi when they returned home from school. I tell you it was just so touching because I got the genuine and sincere sense that they did not want me to leave and that they really would miss me. I do not think it is often, if ever, that people come into their lives who take a genuine interest in them and treat them like they are special. So just doing and experiencing that has certainly helped to make this whole thing worthwhile, and of course that is just the beginning. That is one of the things I wrote you about before I got here, just being able to have that kind of impact. This week I start with the form 3 students for three weeks while they are on their holiday.

Ken, these are the best stories. All of these anecdotes are so touching. You really need to write it all down. You know that you're inspiring so many people with what you are doing. I mean that, I'm honored to be your friend when I read this stuff. Of course, it reminds me of how much I miss you!

As I think I told you before this area is VERY remote. You just can't imagine how people live. I have visited the homes of all my students and it just kind of takes your breath away. It is amazing that some of these kids are able to achieve anything given the barriers that they face. But at the same time it is so sweet because they all want me to come and meet their relatives and have a meal or tea with them. It's like what I said above, I just don't think it is often if ever that these kids have someone in their lives who takes the time to be really interested in them and treat them like intelligent adults. So that is very nice.

I'll say that while not a lot, I do miss being home. I certainly miss you and our catty comments at others' expense and also just talking with someone with whom you have a lot in common and have shared experience. I also just want to hang out with you in New York! In a weird way I do miss the challenge of work, it has been 10 months now. Like you I have not worked out in about three months now, but oh well, I will take care of that when the time comes. Miss some of the small things like in fact my big bed, or I guess civilization in general. I totally miss reading the paper every day, yeah I can get news online (well not the past week, as our phone line was out) but I like the physical paper, especially the Sunday paper. Of course getting news magazines is just about impossible. You would laugh at the bookstores here. The one in Blantyne surprisingly actually had some NYT Top 20 books, but most of the books were used. The one right by the cash register was circa 1974 or so—Pat Boone's Shape Up Your Life *or something like that. I thought if these poor people don't have it bad enough, now they have to be subject to Pat Boone's philosophy...ugh. So I kind of miss all of that. And of course I miss my friends and just being home in general.*

You know what??, not that much is going on. I was gone for two months and no one could think of anything that I missed...which tells me that people are not doing enough memorable things (like you are!).

I also get a little nervous about just exactly what direction my life is going. I love doing this, but as I said I can't help but think to myself if I was foolish in turning down jobs to do this. But I keep telling myself (as others have), rightfully I believe, that there is no way this experience will be bad for me. I honestly needed to do this so badly for my soul and my spirit. It has been weird not having income—just the opposite, in fact. And I think about where I am going to live when I get home and will I move back to San Francisco, will I decide to move back over to Oakland, will I be in the Bay Area at all. What kind of job will I have—what will be available? Will being out of the market be a drawback? How will the market be? I have to say that I like making money and being able to save AND to spend on fun things like frivolous trips and whatnot.

You know, it always amazes me how you and I are so similar...I was alluding to it earlier. But I'm obsessed with the direction I'm taking in life. WHAT THE FUCK AM I DOING? Is the main question.

Here are the issues:

1. Career-wise—keep trying to run my own business—or—get some cushy corporate job?
2. Why can't I find the right guy? And when I do find them, why do I stop being attracted and dump them after two to four years?
3. Should I be settling down, buying a house, raising a family? I would think I want to have kids. Dave and Kim just had a little girl. My family's squeezing out pups like crazy. It just seems like the next step.
4. Do I live in New York or S.F.? I feel fucking disembodied right now. One month in N.Y. and two months in Europe and then returning to S.F. is bizarre. Do I live here?? Where do I want to live? I want to live in New York, but I can't walk away from the business...it's all so interconnected...*sniff*

OK—enough griping.

OK, this has definitely gone on too long. Please don't wait so long to send me E-mail. I miss hearing from you even if it is nothing big.

There are some things I could definitely use and will let you know about that SOON, trust me. I hope everything is going well for you—sounds like it is. I do miss you and look forward to seeing you, probably in the New Year unless you can make it down here before then! We'll get our pathetic out-of-shape bodies back into shape in no time! All for now.

Much love,
Ken

I'm going to start trying to lift really hard for the next two months...but it's not as much fun without you here. In fact, I'm going to the gym right after work today. I want to be big by the time September rolls around. I know I was going to do that before my trip, but I dislocated my shoulder and all that crap.

Overall things are really good. I suppose there are some people who would kill to have my problems—quote-unquote "problems." So I need to get over myself.

San Francisco was chilly for the first few days I was here, but has mellowed to crisp, sunny, 68 degrees or so. I'm going to enjoy my visit here...and I'm certainly not in any hurry to go back to New York for the muggy, hot month of August...plus I've got a couple of weddings and bachelor parties to hit—friends from school.

Please send me more stories about your travels...no E-mail is too long. I'm still working on getting pictures scanned. I promise to send some soon.

Love (and non-smelly affection and kisses and smooches),

Mark

• • •

So what was Mark doing with his life on Sept. 10, 2001? That, of course, depends on whom you talk with. Clearly, from his E-mail exchange with Ken, he was thinking about some changes at The Bingham Group. According to Amanda Mark, he had an offer from a New York City–based advertising agency to buy his company in order to expand its own public relations services. Mark, as part of the deal, would have worked as a consultant out of the company's New York office.

Any change, outside of firings, would have been welcomed by his employees, who by September were growing increasingly frustrated with the boss's globe-trotting. While they were in the office worrying about the shrinking client base, Mark had been checking in from Hawaii, Las Vegas, Monaco, and Pamplona. "At the time we were sitting in the office saying to ourselves, 'What is that man doing?' " says Peer-Olaf Richter, one of Mark's employees. "I think that if it were my office I would at least try to call in every day, if not every other day. But we were hearing less and less from him. He basically didn't tell us anything."

While public relations was certainly in Mark's blood, he was also developing a passion for writing and had talked with Todd Sarner about moving to Paris for a few months or half a year to devote himself to that passion. In preparation for what he hoped would someday be the Great American Novel, he started checking out books on writing from the New York City public library.

One of the books, Amanda remembers, suggested that he write a eulogy for himself. "We talked about this, and about what we wanted written on our tombstones, and we decided that we were going to have to do something that really made a difference," she recalls. "We both agreed that we wanted to be one of those authors who writes a book that kids hate having to study when they are students but then, once they've grown up, are really glad they've read it. That was the goal. We wanted to be remembered."

When Mark mentioned that his family was "squeezing out pups like crazy," he meant specifically his mother. Alice, who

was 51, had given birth to four children since 1999 as a surrogate for her brother Vaughn and sister-in-law Kathy. Mark was
actually on hand for the birth of the first baby, a girl named
Jillian, born on July 4, 1999. "He was there videotaping," Alice
says. "That was something I was worried about throughout the
whole pregnancy. I kept wondering, *How am I ever going to be
able to appear naked in front of my whole family?* I kept telling
Mark, 'No crotch shots!' But believe me, when I was going
through labor that was the last thing I was thinking about."

Mark wasn't on hand when the next three, triplet boys
Harrison, Bryce, and Garrett, were born March 14, 2001. He
was nevertheless thrilled by his new cousins, who included
Savannah, who was carried by another surrogate mother and
was born June 8, 1999. "He was excited and he was sort of
proud that his mom was doing this," Alice says. "But he also
purported to be jealous that, after 29 years of being the only
grandchild, he was suddenly being displaced. He started calling
himself 'the original grandchild,' and asked that we refer to him
as 'Uncle Mark,' because he thought that sounded more important than 'Cousin Mark.'"

Dave and Kim Kupiecki's new baby, Vivian, was born just
two weeks before the triplets, further driving home Mark's
point that starting a family seemed like it should be "the next
step" for him. Family had always been important to Mark, and
he had talked a lot about someday becoming a father. He and
Paul had discussed adoption when they were together. And
when his mother's surrogacy opened his eyes to alternatives in
addition to adoption, Mark toyed with the idea that his Aunt
Candy might someday have his and Joe Cinquini's baby.

"Mark's grandparents didn't know he was gay, and because I
was hanging out so much with his family they thought I had
the hots for Candy," Joe says, laughing. The confusion gave
Mark an idea. "He said, 'Why don't you two have a baby? It
would be part of me and it would be part of you.' I just said,
'Are you out of your mind?' "

Being single changed Mark's family planning, but it didn't change the game plan altogether. "He told me one day, 'You know, Mom, I've been thinking about having children, and Amanda loves me. She'd have my baby,'" Alice says. "I thought, *Whoa! That's a lot of love.*" Amanda acknowledges that she and Mark had talked about that possibility. Their conversation, however, never moved beyond the discussion phase. "I told him I would carry a baby for him when he was ready to have a child," Amanda says. "But only if it was a donor egg. If it was mine I couldn't give it up."

Without a doubt, Mark was on sure footing with his family of friends on September 10. Before he left for Europe in July he and Paul had had several coincidental run-ins with each other in New York City. After the last one, ended up spending the night catching up and, as they had done so many times over dinner when they were a couple, taking stock of each other's lives. "As big as New York is, we ran into each other three nights in a row," Paul says. "The last few hours we were together we just walked around the Village and talked. He talked about the Fog, the people in his life, and definitely about his business. We used to do that every day, or at least had an opportunity to do it every day, so it was wonderful and a relief to get another chance to do it."

Mark also had several poignant encounters with friends in San Francisco after returning home from his run with the bulls. Spencer Kelly hosted a couple of sangria/Pamplona redux parties so everyone could see Mark's videotape from the trip as well as the scar on the back of his leg. "Somewhere around midnight or so after the second party, Mark and a group of the guys decided to go out and hit the bars, and I was tired, so I stayed in," Spencer says. "Whereas most guys usually give you a straight-guy hug when they say goodbye, Mark gave you a huge hug and a peck on the cheek—even if he had to bend down seven inches to do so, like he did with me. Well, he did that that night and then said, 'I love you, man.' That was weird for us, but I felt strangely emotional and told him the same thing."

Mark and Dave Kupiecki got together for a movie and several beers at Pat O'Shea's tavern before Mark headed back to New York City. "He asked me some really weird things that night," Dave says. "He asked me about infidelity and how I felt about it, which was especially weird because I can look anybody in the eye and say that I've never even come remotely close to being unfaithful to Kim. Then he asked me about Vivie and fatherhood and how that had changed things for me. There were so many people who wanted Mark's time and who wanted to be with him," Dave adds. "It was odd that we were able to spend the whole night together—just talking."

Todd Sarner gave Mark a ride to the airport when he left San Francisco for New York the last time. "He called me the night before and said, 'Hey, I was thinking, I have my old Pathfinder that I haven't been using, and I know you need a truck. Why I don't I come by your place tomorrow morning and have you take me to the airport. You can check out the truck while I'm gone. If you like it, I'll sell it to you real cheap. I don't want any weird situation where I sell you a car and then it breaks down,'" Todd says.

The two of them didn't have a particularly deep conversation during the half-hour drive to the airport—they talked a bit about a video project they hoped to collaborate on. However, when they got to the airport, Todd says, "We got out of the truck and I gave him a big hug. I am real grateful to have had that opportunity."

Then, of course, there was the over-the-top weekend Mark, Amanda, and Larry Salmela spent in celebration of Amanda's 31st birthday on September 9. As a result, Mark spent a good deal of September 10 nursing a hangover from the night before. "I came home from work at about 2:30 P.M. because I wasn't feeling very well myself," Amanda says. "And Mark was sitting in his underwear on the couch. He told me that he was going to fly back to San Francisco that night. Then, at about 5:30 P.M.,

I said, 'Shouldn't you be going?' And he told me he had changed his mind and that he was going to stay with Matt Hall that night—because he lived only 20 minutes from the airport—and that he was going to head out in the morning."

Mark met Matt in late June when they were both visiting the America Online chat room "Husky and Stocky M4M." "I saw his screen name, 'BignDumbNY,' and started to read his profile," Matt says. "It said something like, 'Sports, rugby, in New York; not into poppers, leather, or kink, but like vanilla shakes.' Then all of a sudden I got an instant message from BignDumbNY and it scared me half to death. I thought I had accidentally pushed something when I was reading his profile."

After hitting it off online, they agreed to meet in person. And after that was a success they decided to spend a week together in early September at the Southern Decadence festival in New Orleans. "We had nothing in common when we first met, and I remember thinking, *Oh, God, another dumb jock.* Then after a while I started feeling magic develop," Matt says. "Every time we were together it was timeless for me. In New Orleans we didn't even look at our watches. We never even knew what day it was."

Their time together had been romantic, but Matt says they had an understanding that they were to be "just friends." So Matt wasn't expecting anything other than that when he called Mark on September 10 to say hello. "He said he was going to fly out on Tuesday and talked about wanting to come down to my place. So after work, I drove up to Manhattan, we ate some take-out Chinese food as he packed his bag, and then we headed back to my place."

That night at Matt's home in Denville, N.J., the two men ate ice cream, watched *Monday Night Football*, and chatted while Mark trimmed his goatee in front of the bathroom mirror. Then, out of the blue, Mark turned to Matt and asked, "When do we talk about making this relationship more exclusive?"

"I just looked at him and said, 'You need to be on this coast full-time,'" Matt says, admitting that even though Mark's question took him by surprise, he was excited about the possibility of a more serious relationship with him.

And as the two of them went to bed and set the alarm in order to get Mark to the airport in time the next morning, Matt thought of an exchange he and Mark had when they first met. "He asked me one day, 'Matt, what's your passion?' And I blinked my eyes, shook my head, looked at him, and said, 'What?' Then he repeated himself. 'What's your passion in life? What do you want to do? Where do you want to go? Who do you want to be?' I was dumbfounded and just said that I didn't know, and he answered, 'We'll have to figure that out for you.'

"So I threw it back at him and asked, 'What's your passion, Mark?' and he immediately had an answer for me. He said, 'To live life to the fullest, to take advantage of every opportunity, to meet people, to go places, to do what I can with my time on Earth.'"

"*Mark, it's Steven. I'm just calling. I didn't know if you were in New York or not. But I was just calling to make sure you were OK. Give us a call. Leave a message at the house or something. I'll speak to you soon. Bye.*"

"*Hey, Mark. It's Jim. It's 3:30 on Tuesday and I'm really praying you're OK, buddy. I'm worried. Anyway, call me, you know, somewhere. Leave me a message anywhere, anytime. I don't care. Just let me know you're OK. Thanks. I hope you're OK. Bye.*"

"*Hey, Mark. It's Bryce. Please give me a call as soon as you get this message. I hope you're OK. Bye.*"

—the 24th, 25th, and 26th unheard voice-mail messages left on Mark Bingham's mobile phone on Sept. 11, 2001— the first from his friend Steven Gold, the second from an acquaintance named Jim, and the third from his San Francisco Fog teammate Bryce Eberhart

UNITED AIRLINES FLIGHT 93 FINALLY took off from Newark International Airport's Runway 4-Left at 8:42 A.M. on Tuesday, Sept. 11, 2001. In contrast to the confusion on the ground, which had caused the flight's 42-minute delay, the sky that morning was quiet and clear. And as the Boeing 757 banked left along the Hudson River and headed west toward San Francisco, the sun's intensity was the only thing that could have hindered the view of lower Manhattan and its signature World Trade Center towers for Mark and the other passengers on the righthand side of the plane. They may have even seen the dot in the distance that was American Airlines Flight 11. The Boeing 767 crashed into the World Trade Center's north tower just three minutes after Flight 93 took off from Newark International.

Mark's flight was well beyond Manhattan by that point, however, and its seven-member crew was preparing for another routine flight across the country. Of the five United Airlines flight attendants on board, Wanda Green and Lorraine Bay were stationed in first class. As they introduced themselves to Mark, Tom Burnett, and the other passengers in the front cabin—which included four Middle Eastern–looking men—they handed out menus and explained that breakfast would be a choice between an omelet and a fruit plate.

At about 9:06 A.M., as United Airlines Flight 175 slammed

into the World Trade Center's south tower, Deborah Welsh, who is believed to have been the purser on Flight 93, was probably announcing to the cabin that the in-flight movie that morning was *A Knight's Tale,* starring Heath Ledger.

In the 24 minutes that Flight 93 had been in the air, life on the ground had been altered more than most of the 44 people on board could have ever imagined. And it would be at least another 25 minutes before they would know anything about it.

The only notice that the plane's captain, Jason Dahl, and his first officer, LeRoy Homer, had received to indicate something was amiss was a message that flashed across the cockpit computer screen shortly after 9 A.M. It read: "Beware, cockpit intrusion." Either Dahl or LeRoy typed "Confirmed" in response.

At 9:25, as the jet approached the outskirts of Cleveland, Dahl made his first and only contact with air-traffic control in the city. "Good morning," he said. Just as Dahl radioed Cleveland, four men in first class—Ziad Samir Jarrahi, Ahmed Alhaznawi, Ahmed Alnami, and Saeed Alghamdi—started to put red bandannas on their heads.

It's likely that this was not the first time these men, who all looked as if they were in their 20s or early 30s, had caught the attention of the others on the plane. As Mark and the other passengers shuffled through their morning newspapers and bantered with the flight attendants, these men could not be bothered. They didn't have time. For if they were following instructions, each of them had to silently pray "There is no God but God" 1,000 times before putting on their bandannas.

Then, at 9:28 A.M., an air-traffic-controller heard a quick scream and the sound of a struggle coming from Flight 93 and asked, "Did somebody call Cleveland?" After 40 seconds of dead air in response, the air-traffic controller heard one of the United pilots scream, "Get out of here! Get out of here!"

What happened in the next couple of minutes is unclear, since the tape recovered from Flight 93's cockpit voice recorder, which recorded on a continuous loop for a half-hour, doesn't start until shortly after 9:30 A.M. It begins with the sound of a woman, most likely a flight attendant, pleading for her life. Gurgling and choking noises also can be heard and are assumed to be coming from Dahl and Homer, who were struggling either to say something or to breathe.

It's also unclear exactly how the hijackers broke into the cockpit. They could have simply barged in, since the cockpit door was designed only to withstand 150 pounds of pressure. Or they may have forced a flight attendant to let them in. Either way, it's widely believed that Jarrahi and one of the other hijackers forced their way into the cockpit and used either knives or box cutters to slash the throats of both Dahl and Homer. The other two hijackers, meanwhile, divided the passengers and flight attendants into two groups and split them between the plane's front and back cabins. They were both armed with knives, and one had what he said was a bomb strapped to his body.

It's also not clear if Mark was in the front or the back of the plane at this point. Jarrahi, who is believed to have been flying the plane, tried to calm the passengers by making an announcement that ended up going to Cleveland air-traffic control rather than throughout the plane. "Hi, this is the captain," he said in a heavily accented and winded voice that suggested he was attempting to catch his breath after his struggle with Dahl and Homer. "We'd like you to all remain seated. There is a bomb on board. We are going to return to the airport. And they have our demands, so please remain quiet."

But the passengers and the flight attendants did not remain quiet. Instead they telephoned their loved ones using the GTE Airfones on the plane and, in some cases, their own mobile phones. Mark called his mother at his Aunt Kathy and Uncle Vaughn's home, where she was helping to care for their newborn boys.

Alice, who was in her room with baby Garrett, heard the

phone ring at 6:44 A.M. Pacific time. But the phone in her room wasn't working, so she assumed Carol Phipps, a family friend who was also there to help with the babies, would pick it up in another room. After a series of rings, the phone stopped. Then, when it started ringing a second time, Carol picked it up. "Get Kathy or Alice quickly," Mark said in a muffled voice. "Is this Lee?" Carol asked, referring to another of Mark's uncles. "No," he said, and then again pleaded, "Get Kathy or Alice quickly."

Alice then heard Carol pad quickly down the ranch-style home's long hallway to Kathy and Vaughn's bedroom and then knew something was wrong when she heard Kathy run to the phone. Alice got out of bed herself and, as she approached Kathy, heard her say, "I love you too, Mark. Let me get your mom."

"When she saw me, she said, 'Alice, come talk to Mark. He's been hijacked,'" Alice recalls. "Then she handed me the phone and a piece of paper that had 'Flight 93' and 'United' written on it. I took the phone and—oh, I can't remember what I said—but I heard Mark say, 'Mom, this is Mark Bingham.' It wasn't until Mark used his last name that Alice was hit with the weight of what Kathy had just told her.

"I found out later from Kathy that Mark had said he wanted to let us know that he loved us—in case he never saw us again. He didn't say anything about not seeing me again when we talked, though. What he did say was, 'I just want to tell you that I love you. I'm on a flight from Newark to San Francisco and there are three guys on board and they have taken over the plane and they say they have a bomb.' At some point he added, 'I'm calling you from the Airfone,' and then asked, 'You believe me, don't you, Mom?'

"'Yes Mark, I believe you,' I said. 'Who are these guys?' Then he was interrupted by someone who was speaking in a low-toned male voice that, by its cadence, sounded like it was speaking English. I just heard these muffled voices for about 30 seconds, and I kept hoping Mark would come back on the phone.

"When he did come back, he repeated, 'I'm calling you with an Airfone.' I remember that distinctly because I knew Airfones are pretty conspicuous things, and I was afraid he would bring attention to himself and that the hijackers were going to pull him out of his seat and kill him. But I didn't express that to him. I just asked him again, 'Who are these guys?' After another long pause he came back and asked again, 'You believe me, don't you, Mom?' And that was the extent of our conversation. There was another long, agonizing pause, and I could hear ambient noise. But then the phone just trailed off."

No one at the Hoglan home yet knew the fate of the other American airliners, the third of which—American Airlines Flight 77—had crashed into the Pentagon at 9:45 A.M., a minute after Mark had placed the call to his mother. When it became clear that Alice's phone call with Mark was indeed over, Vaughn turned on the TV to see if there was any news of the hijacking. The family immediately saw taped footage of what turned out to be United Flight 175 crashing into the south tower of the World Trade Center.

"When I heard from Mark that his plane had been hijacked, I thought it was going to be a long, agonizing wait, but that [the hijackers] would eventually release him," Alice says. "And then I saw Flight 175 hit the World Trade Center." Alice knew in her gut, even before she heard the details of what she was watching, that it hadn't been Mark's plane that was crashing on TV. *How could it be?* she asked herself. *He was just on the phone with me.* But what that footage immediately confirmed was that what was happening to her son was not going to be a typical hijacking, if there could be such a thing.

What, if anything, could she do? "We just cast about, Vaughn and Kathy and I," Alice says. "Then Vaughn came up with a couple of good ideas." He told Alice to call the FBI, who asked her a series of questions about the hijackers that she couldn't answer. He also suggested she try to call Mark back on his mobile phone to let him know the full scope of the terrorist attack he was now a part of. If Mark had the information about the fate of the other flights, Vaughn reasoned, perhaps he and the other passengers on Flight 93 could wrest control of the plane from the hijackers and save their own lives—not to mention countless other lives on the ground.

Alice made two phone calls to Mark's mobile phone, neither of which were answered. She left a message both times. In the first she said:

"Mark, this is your mom. It's 10:54 A.M. [Eastern time]. The news is that it's been hijacked by terrorists. They are planning to probably use the plane as a target to hit some site on the ground. So if you possibly can, try to overpower these guys if you can—'cause they will probably use the plane as a target. I would say go ahead and do everything you can to overpower them, because they're hell-bent. You know the number here. OK, I love you sweetie. Bye."

In the second message, she reiterated her point:

"Mark, apparently it's terrorists and they're hell-bent on crashing the aircraft. So if you can, try to take over the aircraft. [*fumbling for words*] There doesn't seem to be much plan to land the aircraft normally. So I guess your best bet would be to try to take it over, if you can. Or tell the other passengers. There's one flight that they say is headed toward San Francisco. It might be yours. So, if you can, group some people and perhaps do the best you can to get control of it. I love you, sweetie. Good luck. Bye-bye."

It would be impossible for a mother to prepare herself for the kind of horrifying situation Alice faced that morning. Yet, with the exception of a couple instances where she said something other than she'd intended—"I miscalculated the time from Pacific to Eastern and actually made the call at 9:54 A.M.," she says. "And I meant to say they planned to use the plane as 'a weapon' rather than as 'a target' "—Alice's messages reflect a composure few mothers might imagine themselves having in the same situation.

"There's no doubt I was worried, but I was trying to think about what could be done rather than what was likely to happen," Alice says. "We were still very hopeful too. Vaughn and Kathy and I were hopeful that since the terrorists had already accomplished a truly ugly thing, perhaps they would land Mark's plane safely."

Mark never got the messages his mother left on his mobile phone, but there is no doubt he got the information she was trying to pass on to him through other passengers who also made phone calls to their loved ones.

Tom Burnett made four phone calls to his wife, Deena Burnett, at their home in San Ramon, Calif. In the first he told her that the hijackers had knifed a man. Then, when he called back a second time, he told Deena that the man who had been knifed was now dead. Deena informed Tom about the attack at the World Trade Center, and then he asked her a series of questions about the attack. "I could tell Tom was formulating a plan because of the way he was trying to put it all together, and that had sort of a calming effect, because he sounded so clearheaded," Deena told *Rolling Stone* magazine.

When Tom called a third time, Deena told him about the Pentagon. He again asked questions and then concluded, "I don't think they have a bomb. I think they're just telling us that for crowd control." In his final call, it was evident he and at least some of the other passengers had formulated a plan. "A group of us is going to do something," he said. When Deena protested, urging her husband not to draw attention to himself, he said, "Deena, they're going to run this plane into a building somewhere in Washington. We've got to do something. If they're going to crash this plane, we've got to do something."

Jeremy Glick, a 31-year-old former national judo champion

from New Jersey, also telephoned his wife, Lyz Glick, and told her that the passengers were going to take a vote over whether they should stage an attack against the hijackers. And Todd Beamer, a 32-year-old who had graduated from Los Gatos High School the year before Mark, talked with operator Lisa Jefferson when he couldn't reach his wife, Lisa Beamer. He too said the passengers had decided their only chance for survival was to fight back. Flight attendant Sandy Bradshaw, meanwhile, called her husband, Phil Bradshaw, in Greensboro, N.C., and said she and several other flight attendants were filling coffeepots with boiling water to throw at the hijackers. And flight attendant CeeCee Lyles, who telephoned her husband, Lorne Lyles, in Fort Myers, Fla., said, the passengers were "getting ready to force their way in the cockpit."

Deena Burnett later told Alice Hoglan that during one of her phone conversations with her husband, Tom, she heard a heavy pounding sound in the background. "When she asked what it was, Tom told her, 'That's my seatmate. He's trying to get somebody out from hiding in the bathroom to help us,' " Alice says. "Tom Burnett was talking about Mark."

Meanwhile, the two terrorists in the cockpit were having trouble controlling the plane. Their difficulty started when they turned off the autopilot shortly after storming the front of the plane. As if it were an automobile at cruising speed that was suddenly downshifted, the plane staggered in midair. The cockpit recorder also picked up a series of clicks that sound as if the hijackers were nervously and perhaps randomly pushing buttons and flipping switches throughout the cockpit.

According to air-traffic control records, the jet U-turned over Ohio before making a beeline for what appeared to be Washington, D.C., first flying over part of West Virginia and then heading into Pennsylvania. Its erratic flight path over West Virginia, during which the plane made a series of sharp turns, suggests the hijackers were trying to knock the now-rowdy passengers off their feet. According to the conversations they had with their families, the passengers and flight attendants knew that the plane was flying southeast and, understanding what had already happened at the World Trade Center and the Pentagon, assumed they were heading toward a target in Washington, D.C. The first clear indication of their uprising on the cockpit voice recorder came at 9:55 A.M., when one of the hijackers in the cockpit suggests that the other two be let in for their own safety.

Just before 9:57 A.M., Sandy Bradshaw told her husband, "We're running to first class now." Operator Lisa Jefferson heard Todd Beamer say, "Let's roll." And CeeCee Lyles, who was still on the phone with her husband, screamed, "They're doing it! They're doing it! They're doing it!" Then, at exactly 9:57 A.M., the cockpit voice recorder picked up the sounds of what was the first counterattack in the war on terrorism: Crashing galley dishes and a distinctly male American voice shouting, "Let's get them!"

Obviously rattled, one terrorist suggested cutting oxygen off outside the cockpit. Another can be heard on the cockpit voice recorder saying, "Take it easy." Still another voice suggested scrapping the mission and crashing the plane. Their scheming was interrupted by another male English-speaking voice, although it is unclear whether the passenger had broken into the cockpit or was just on the other side of the door. Obviously unprepared for what had befallen them, the terrorists seem to have panicked and started to fight for control of the jet, with one of them shouting, "Give it to me!" at 10 A.M.

At 10:06 the cockpit voice recorder catches its last voice— one of the terrorists screaming, *"Allah akbar!"* (God is great).

Now in a steep dive, the 757's wings tipped back and forth like a seesaw, according to eyewitnesses on the ground. And as it crashed into a rolling field in rural Somerset County, Pa., the jet, which was traveling faster than 570 miles per hour at the end, exploded into a fireball and created a crater 50 feet deep. Flight 93 ended at 10:06 A.M., an hour and 24 minutes after it left

Newark International Airport, 22 minutes after Mark telephoned his mother, and 12 minutes after Alice left the two desperate voice-mail messages on her son's mobile phone.

· · ·

Alice's messages were two of the 44 she was able to retrieve from Mark's AT&T mobile phone account several months after the attack on September 11. There were probably many more messages left on Mark's phone that day. But as a result of the nation's overburdened communications network on September 11, some of them were not actually recorded. Amanda Mark, for example, says she left several messages on Mark's mobile phone, but only one made it to his voice-mail.

Played in order, the messages serve as a sort of seismograph, measuring the confusion, horror, and despair Mark's family and friends—and indeed, many people around the world—experienced that day. The first messages are fast and fragmented, as though the people leaving them were scrambling to make sense of the situation and find the words to convey the gravity of the emergency. "Looking at this big wreck," Mark's father said, as he tried to stop himself from sobbing. "My God, this is just devastating," Ken Montgomery said. "I just can't believe this."

Amanda just wanted to know where her roommate was. "Where are you? Call me, please," she said. When she left that message, Amanda, who works for Morgan Stanley in midtown Manhattan, was also busy determining the whereabouts of her coworkers, at least one of whom was in the World Trade Center for training that morning. "At about 9:30 or 9:40 [between 10 and 20 minutes before the first tower collapsed], I was telling him to get the fuck out of there," she says. "And my boss told me I was overreacting." Once she gathered everyone, she took those who lived outside Manhattan and therefore couldn't go home to the apartment she and Mark shared in Chelsea.

Amanda knew Mark was planning to fly out of Newark that morning. And when she heard about Flight 93, she knew he was on that plane. "I, of course, hoped that he was on the earlier flight, but I know Mark. He would have slept in as long as he could and gone for the later morning flight, which was [Flight 93]," she says. She wasn't convinced enough that she didn't call, however. And she tried Alice too. It was Alice who finally answered by the middle of the day and confirmed her fear. Yes, Alice told Amanda. Mark had called her and he was on that flight.

The next messages show how the tragedy forced the callers to second-guess themselves. Nothing in the world was as it was supposed to that day. Mark told most of his friends that he wasn't going to fly home until late in the week. But they couldn't be sure. The messages also are a testament to persistence. When Mark didn't answer their first calls, they dialed and dialed again until they could get through. "Hey, Mark. This is Mary, Damon's mom," Mary Billian said in the message she left when her son hadn't heard back from leaving his own message. "Just trying to check up and to make sure that you and Amanda are OK."

Steven Gold had to work late September 11, but he made every effort to stay on top of the day's news. Still, he didn't give a second thought to Mark's safety until his partner, Bill Hollywood, called him at about 2 P.M. and asked if Mark was supposed to be flying that day. "I immediately told him no, because I knew that Mark wasn't supposed to be heading back until the end of the week," Steven says. "But of course then I started to worry." In his first voice-mail message, Steven said, almost calmly, "I didn't know if you were in New York or not. But I was just calling to make sure you were OK. Give us a call." The second was a bit more urgent, however. "I was just hoping that I could get in touch with you," he said. "Bill and I are a little worried about you. Give us a call as soon as you get this. Let us know you're OK."

It wasn't unusual for Steven to get Mark's voice-mail when

he called, but it was unusual not to get a call in return. So when he was headed home at about 8 P.M., he called Mark and Amanda's apartment. "I asked to speak to Amanda, and the person who answered said she couldn't come to the phone. Then I said, 'Actually, I want to speak to Mark,' and Amanda came to the phone. As soon as she said 'Hello,' I knew."

Just as Steven knew from Amanda's voice, the last messages left on Mark's voice-mail that day indicate a sense of knowing as well. Just a series of hang-ups, they are a kind of technological coda—a confirmation that Mark's life had really ended.

"Hey, Mark. It's Steven. I was just hoping that I could get in touch with you. Bill and I are a little worried about you. Give us a call as soon as you get this."

"Mark, this is Tom Bilbo. I was just giving you a call. I wanted to see if you're OK. I heard your name or someone with your name mentioned on the news, and I just want to try to and get a hold of you. Anyway, I'll try and reach you later. Bye."

"Hey, Mark. This is John. I was just calling to see what you were up to. You can reach me at home. Thanks. Bye."

—the 27th, 28th, and 29th unheard voice-mail messages left on Mark Bingham's mobile phone on Sept. 11, 2001— the first from his friend Steven Gold, the second from his friend Tom Bilbo, and the third from his friend John

"ALICE WAS IT FOR MARK. HE TOOK care of her. He protected her at all times," Todd Sarner says. "I think he was still protecting her on that flight that day. He was sitting next to Tom Burnett and they were talking about what was going on, but he never told Alice that [when he called] because he was protecting her." Todd, like almost everyone who knew Mark, says that when he heard about the fate of Flight 93 he knew right away that Mark was among the passengers who helped foil the terrorists' ultimate plan for the plane. He says that one of the most frustrating things he's experienced since September 11 has been knowing "more than anything I've known in my life" that Mark was involved in taking the plane down—but then not knowing how to adequately explain how he knows.

"I keep having this image from watching Mark play rugby a couple years ago," he says. "His team had just kicked the ball, and there were probably 15 people between Mark and the guy who caught it. And I just remember watching Mark do something I've seen him do a thousand times—duck down his head and go through the crowd fearlessly, like he wasn't even there, and then tackle that guy."

No one knows for sure what happened on Flight 93 that morning and what ultimately caused the plane to crash in Somerset County, Pa. Seven months after the attack, the family members of the passengers and crew on board were allowed to hear the cockpit voice recording but were asked by investigators not to reveal the specifics of what they heard and to say no more than they did—that the tape confirmed that their loved ones acted heroically. Still, the people who knew Mark Bingham best say they have all the proof they need.

Mark's former boss Holland Carney remembers the time Mark came to work with two black eyes after thwarting an attempted mugging in San Francisco. "What the fuck?" he told her at the time. "If these guys jump me, I'm not going to take it." And Amanda Mark can't help but recall Mark's first home football game. Although so many of his fraternity brothers had decided to tackle the University of Wisconsin mascot, when it came time to actually jump on the field, Mark was the only one who did it.

As ordinary a guy as Mark was, friends say there was a part of him that was a little unlike the rest of us. While most people's reaction to danger is often delayed by shock, Mark's was immediate and head-on. He didn't weigh his options, because in his mind there often were no options. It's a characteristic Amanda thinks was passed on by Mark's mother—who, as much as she delighted in her son's desire to protect her, is a very strong woman in her own right.

"I learned how amazing Alice is the first time I came to California in 1989. We were driving down Interstate 5 on our way to Lake Arrowhead when we saw a car on fire on the side of the road," Amanda says. As full as the freeway was with traffic, nobody stopped to help the people with the burning car. But "Alice pulled over, had us pull all of the luggage out of the trunk, grabbed a fire extinguisher, and put out the fire. And you wonder where Mark got his fire?"

Within hours of the crash of Flight 93, officials in Washington, D.C., said it was almost certain, as Tom Burnett had told his wife, Deena, that the terrorists were directing the plane toward a target in Washington, D.C., most likely the

Capitol Building or the White House. (Based on further investigation, government officials said eight months after the attack that the hijackers had intended to smash the Boeing 757 into the White House.)

Armed with this information, several congressional officials immediately singled Flight 93's passengers and crew for recognition. Pennsylvania's U.S. senators, Arlen Specter and Rick Santorum, suggested to their colleagues on Capitol Hill that the Congressional Medal of Honor—the highest award a civilian can receive—be awarded to Mark and the others on the flight. "There's a deep sense of gratitude," Specter said. And as 7,000 people gathered on September 17 for an interfaith service in San Francisco, Senator Barbara Boxer of California honored Mark by presenting a U.S. flag to Mark's friend and former partner Paul Holm. Then, on September 22, Arizona senator John McCain gave a tearful eulogy at a memorial service held at Cal-Berkeley for Mark.

Although he was apolitical by most accounts and libertarian by others, Mark supported McCain, a Republican, in his 2000 bid for the White House, because the senator's maverick style appealed to him. The two met briefly for a photo-op during a fundraiser, and Mark displayed the photograph in his office. McCain accepted Alice's invitation to the service and gave the following eulogy:

> I didn't know Mark Bingham. We met once, briefly, during my presidential campaign, yet I cannot say that I knew him well. But I wish I had. You meet a lot of people when you run for president. I was fortunate to have had the support of many Americans who were, until then, strangers to me. And I regret to say that, like most candidates, I was preoccupied with winning or losing. I had not thought as much as I should have about what an honor, what an extraordinary honor it was to have so many citizens of the greatest nation on Earth place their

trust in me, and use our campaign as an expression of their own patriotism. They were the best thing about our campaign, not me. Had I been successful, my greatest challenge would have been to prove myself worthy of the faith of so many good people.

I love my country, and I take pride in serving her. But I cannot say that I love her more or as well as Mark Bingham did, or the other heroes on United Flight 93 who gave their lives to prevent our enemies from inflicting an even greater injury on our country. It has been my fate to witness great courage and sacrifice for America's sake, but none greater than the selfless sacrifice of Mark Bingham and those good men who grasped the gravity of the moment, understood the threat, and decided to fight back at the cost of their lives.

In the Gospel of John it is written "Greater lover hath no man than this, that a man may lay down his life for his friends." Such was the love that Mark and his comrades possessed, as they laid down their lives for others. A love so sublime that only God's love surpasses it.

It is now believed that the terrorists on Flight 93 intended to crash the airplane into the United States Capitol, where I work, the great house of democracy where I was that day. It is very possible that I would have been in the building, with a great many other people, when that fateful, terrible moment occurred and a beautiful symbol of our freedom was destroyed, along with hundreds if not thousands of lives. I may very well owe my life to Mark and the others who summoned the enormous courage and love necessary to deny those depraved, hateful men their terrible triumph. Such a debt you incur for life.

I will try very hard, very hard, to discharge my public duties in a manner that honors their memory. All public servants are now solemnly obliged to do all we can to help this nation remain worthy of sacrifice of the brave passengers on Flight 93.

No American living today will ever forget what happened on Sept. 11, 2001. That day was the moment when the hinge of history swung toward a new era, not only in the affairs of this nation, but in the affairs of all humanity. The opening chapter of this new history is tinged with great sadness and uncertainty. But as we begin, please take strength from the example of the American we honor today, and those who perished to save others in New York, Washington, and Pennsylvania. The days ahead will be difficult, and we will know more loss and sorrow. But we will prevail. We will prevail.

Pay no heed to the voices of the poor, misguided souls in this country and overseas, who claim that America brought these atrocities on herself. They are deluded, and their hearts are cramped by hatred and fear. Our respect for man's God-given rights to life, liberty, and the pursuit of happiness assures us a victory even as it made us a target for the enemies of freedom who mistake hate and depravity for power. The losses we have suffered are grave and must not be forgotten. But we should all take pride and unyielding resolve from the knowledge that we were attacked because we were good, and good we will remain as we vanquish the evil that preys upon us.

I never knew Mark Bingham. But I wish I had. I know he was a good son and friend, a good rugby player, a good American, and an extraordinary human being. He supported me, and his support now ranks among the greatest honors of my life. I wish I had known before September 11 just how great an honor his trust in me was. I wish I could have thanked him for it more profusely than time and circumstances allowed. But I know it now. And I thank him with the only means I possess, by being as good an American as he was.

America will overcome these atrocities. We will pre-vail over our enemies. We will right this terrible injus-tice. And when we do, let us claim it as a tribute to our liberty, and to Mark Bingham and all those who died to defend it.

To all of you who loved Mark, and were loved by him, he will never be so far from you that you cannot feel his love. As our faith informs us, you will see him again, when our loving God reunites us all with the loved ones who preceded us. Take care of each other until then, as he would want you to. May God bless Mark. And may God bless us all. Thank you.

Many newspapers around the world as well as The Associated Press reported Mark's sexual orientation as a part of their September 11 coverage. Yet most politicians, like McCain, decided against mentioning it when recognizing his heroism— seeming to assume the position that Mark was a hero who just happened to be gay. Others, such as former New York City mayor Rudolph Giuliani and New York governor George Pataki, chose to highlight Mark's efforts on Flight 93 and the fact that he was gay as one of the reasons to support gay-rights legislation. Pataki called Mark a "true hero" as he pledged his support for the Sexual Orientation Non-Discrimination Act that was working its way through the state legislature.

While McCain's and Pataki's approaches are hardly con-flicting, they help illustrate questions that arose for others who set out to honor Mark: Is it wrong to highlight the sexual ori-entation of a man who tried not to make a big deal of it when he was alive? Or does trumpeting a gay hero's sexual orienta-tion help everyone by tearing down stereotypes?

Taking it a step further, can a gay man who doesn't consider his sexual orientation a priority be rightfully considered a gay hero? If so, by calling him a hero does one in some way suggest that he is more heroic because he is "less gay"?

On the flip side, how can you treat a man's sexual orientation as equal to his other characteristics if you don't at least mention it? And, indeed, how do you tear down stereotypes without inadvertently suggesting that the activity being stereotyped is somehow embarrassing or needing to be disproved?

Posed side by side, the questions are dizzying. Yet they underscore some of the conflicts when it comes to identifying Mark Bingham as either a "gay hero" or a "hero who happens to be gay." So does a letter sent to *The Advocate* when the national gay and lesbian news magazine named Mark "Person of the Year" in January 2002:

> Bingham was certainly courageous. But his being gay had nothing to do with his decisions and actions. If *The Advocate* is going to select a Person of the Year at all, I would think it would be someone who advanced equality, justice, and nondiscrimination. Choosing Bingham is a slight to all those who really do something for gay rights and a slight against Bingham himself. Because I am quite certain he didn't do what he did because he was gay or that he even stopped to think about his sexuality when making his decisions. He took the actions he did because, gay or straight, he was a man of courage. Shame on you for not selecting someone whose actions and courage actually had something to do with their being queer!

Perhaps the bigger question is one Mark may have posed himself, "Can't you be a hero—or even a gay hero—by simply being yourself?"

Mark's friends have chosen to honor his life by talking about it as often as they can with as many people as possible. "There were thousands of people who died that day," Dave Kupiecki says. "And maybe I'm a little bit selfish about wanting my friend's name in every magazine and in every newspaper.

But my therapy is having people know about him. I know every single person is special on this earth and every one is really unique, but Mark really had something."

To that end, Dave and many of Mark's other close friends have established the Mark Bingham Leadership Fund, which awards an $8,000-$10,000 scholarship to a different Cal-Berkeley student every year. "We're interested in people who can write a good essay about leadership, can show a commitment to social ability, and who don't spend all their time studying," Dave says. "But if you're also a gay rugby player who goes to Cal, you're going to have a pretty good shot at the scholarship."

Meanwhile, Mark's teammates from the San Francisco Fog have instituted the Mark Kendall Bingham Cup Invitational Rugby Tournament and Festival, which now serves as the world championship of gay rugby football. The first tournament, which was staged in June 2002 and included more than 200 participants, was won by the Fog, who had never won a game when Mark was alive. The team now keeps the two-foot-tall Bingham Cup until the next champion is named.

Alice, who was on hand to award the Bingham Cup, has become one of the most vocal Flight 93 family members since September 11. She has been featured on most national TV news programs and is considered by many journalists as a spokesperson for the flight as news continues to break regarding the terrorist attacks or airline and airport safety procedures. She also has taken it upon herself to publish a newsletter that she E-mails to other Flight 93 family members on nearly a weekly basis.

"People have asked me if I would like closure and to be at rest," Alice said on CNN in May. "The truth is that I want to go to my death tortured by the events of September 11. If there is something that I can do to speak out for such issues as an increase in aviation safety [or] a healing of the international tensions that have in some way brought about the events of

September 11, I want to do those things. I do not want to truly be at peace."

Her most determined effort to honor her son's life, however, is much more personal than any issue or concern that could be connected to the fateful day that so powerfully touched the lives of every American. As Alice returns to many of the routines of her life before September 11—including her job as a flight attendant for United Airlines—she is also trying to live in a manner that Mark would have wanted her to.

"One of Mark's biggest frustrations was that he couldn't get his mother to do the simplest things technologically," she explains. "And since I no longer have Mark and I've lost my tech support, I have a renewed commitment to thrust myself into the 20th century now that it's the 21st century. I'm learning how to pull my mail off the Internet, how to go to Web sites, and how to keep my cell phone on. I'm also taking a class in Photoshop."

As if that weren't enough to make her son proud, Alice has—in what most of Mark's friends would say is true Bingham style—even one-upped her son in a number of his life's pursuits. After learning how much Mark loved watching the torch relay in the 2000 Olympics in Sydney, she herself ran with the torch before the 2002 Winter Games in Salt Lake City. "It was an embarrassingly short run that left me breathless," she says of her leg in the relay.

With her winded torch run behind her, Alice put herself through a jogging regimen around Redwood Estates before June 30, 2002, when she marched the length of the San Francisco pride parade surrounded by the 200-plus ruggers in the Bingham Cup tournament. And even though she knows that her son was never very political—especially when it came to his sexual orientation—Alice has enrolled in a public speaking class and has spoken out in favor of equal rights for gay men and lesbians in assignments before her classmates and in front of the board of directors for the gay-rights group Human Rights Campaign.

"Amanda says that it was a real surprise for most of Mark's friends when they learned that he was gay, and that it forced them to rethink a lot of their attitudes," Alice says. "I know that's exactly what happened to me. When I found out that the person I loved most in the world was gay, it was a call to action for me. It was the start of a start of a significant journey for me. And I'm still on it.

"I know that Mark, in many ways, created himself," Alice continues. "In just as many ways, when I think about the way he turned out, I just wonder how I ever got to be his mother."

Acknowledgments

Thank you to Mark Bingham's friends and loved ones for sharing their memories; to Angela Brown, Tiffany Watson, Terri Fabris, Matt Sams, and Judy Wieder at Alyson for their help throughout the publication process; to Victoria Scanlan Stefanakos for her ear; and to Sean Moran for his patience and support.